MANAGING RISK

for projects and programmes

a risk management handbook

MANAGING RISK

for projects and programmes

a risk management handbook

John Bartlett
BA (Hons), LTCL, FAPM (CPM), FRSA

Project Manager Today
P U B L I C A T I O N S

Project Manager Today Publications
Larchdrift Projects Ltd, Unit 12, Moor Place Farm, Plough Lane, Bramshill,
Hook, Hampshire RG27 0RF

First published in Great Britain 2002

ISBN 1 900391 10 4

Bartlett, John
   Managing risk for projects and programmes : a risk
   management handbook
   1. Project management   2. Risk management
   I. Title
   658.4'04
   ISBN 1900391104

Printed and bound in Great Britain
by Intype London Limited

Acknowledgements

I am especially grateful to Dr David Hillson, Director of Consultancy, Project Management Professional Solutions Ltd, for writing the Foreword to this book; also to Richard Watson, BSc(Eng), CEng, MICE, for reviewing the manuscript and providing valuable suggestions from his experience in engineering risk management.

I am particularly grateful to the many people at NCR who have given me encouragement and who have sponsored a firm interest in risk management, without which it would have been difficult to write this book. In particular I would like to thank Jan Burke, Lynne Cantor, Lou Ann McElyea, Bill Gendron and Tim Davis; also Andrew Burrell for reading the entire manuscript and making helpful comments.

I also acknowledge the support of my publishers, whose faith in the project management profession and discipline is unfailing.

John Bartlett

Foreword

The word 'risk' has entered the public consciousness in a new way recently, following terrorist outrages, public health scares and outbreaks of infectious animal diseases. We hear the term from politicians, businessmen, newscasters, social workers, military advisers, journalists, doctors — everywhere people seem to be highlighting the risks we face in all aspects of life. But it appears that less is being said about 'risk management', the process by which we can understand the risks to which we are exposed, and then act appropriately.

Risk management is particularly important for projects and programmes, since they are specifically designed to take risks. The combination of uniqueness, constraints, assumptions, stakeholder expectations, changing environment, and human behaviour all conspire to make projects and programmes risky ventures. As a result, those of us involved with projects and programmes must inevitably come to terms with how to make risk management work if we are to stand any chance of meeting our objectives. If anyone should know about risk and its management, it should be project and programme managers and their teams.

And yet the field of project and programme management is littered with failures, as unforeseen events and circumstances strike home with depressing regularity. Surely we can do better than this? Is 'unforeseen' the same as 'unforeseeable'? Are we doomed to repeat the failures of the past indefinitely? Can risk management ever be effective, making a positive contribution to achievement of objectives, focusing attention on key areas requiring management attention, and maximising the chances of project and programme success?

It is at this point that John Bartlett's book should make a difference. We don't need new theories or techniques or tools in order to make risk management effective. Instead, we need practical guidelines on how to make it work. Drawing on his wide experience as a project and programme manager, John offers advice from the battlefield. His 'view from the trenches' will help others to know what to expect before they go over the top, and will prepare them for what lies ahead. This book will be valuable for the hard-pressed project or programme manager who knows that he or she is at risk, and wants to know what to do about it.

Often too much effort is spent on risk identification and analysis, leaving managers like rabbits caught in the headlights, seeing what is coming towards them but seemingly unable to react. The message of this book is a call to risk management, offering practical and proven methods to respond to risk appropriately and effectively. Putting the contents into practice will certainly help to manage risks on projects and programmes, and hopefully start to reverse the tide of failure which has become all too familiar. Paraphrasing Einstein, if you always do what you've always done, you'll always get what you always got. It is possible to do things differently and deal proactively with project and programme risk – this book shows you how.

Dr David Hillson, FAPM, PMP, MIRM, MCMI
Director, PMProfessional Solutions

Preface

In my frequent role as a project auditor I have seen many interpretations of risk management in projects – some of these have been good and some have been poor. In many cases, project teams seem to be inventing and re-inventing risk management processes, such that there is little consistency of practice. Project management methodologies all extol the virtues of good risk management but rarely show how it should be tackled in practice. This often leaves project teams very much in the dark when it comes to applying risk management for positive effect.

My current view is that, on the whole, risk management is tackled badly in projects and often ranked below other project elements in importance, such as the project plan, resource plan and status reporting. Small wonder then that we continually hear of projects failing.

What I'm finding is a series of inconsistent practices in the name of risk management, many of which are ineffectual in actually reducing risk. I find that project managers become stuck in a high, medium, low mentality in terms of assessing risk, or are expressing risks using only one or two words. I also find that much time is spent recording risks but little time spent in showing real progress in risk mitigation.

It is almost as if some project teams are paying lip service to the universally recognised view that risk management should be undertaken on projects, without understanding the true value of doing so. Yet, risk management practised well should be able to reduce significantly the chances of cost overruns, gross margin erosion, scope creep and a host of other typical project impacts.

The big problem is that project managers are often poor risk managers. The two roles require quite different mindsets. The single-minded task manager is quite different from the lateral-thinking risk identifier. Yet project management methodologies expect the project manager to manage project risk; so why should we be surprised when risk management is not given the attention it deserves?

This book attempts to address the generally poor attention given to risk in projects and programmes. It aims to provide the reader with a sufficient understanding of the subject in order to practise consistently good risk management. It also shows why risk management should be the premier focus for project managers, over and above the other project management elements. It is not a book about the history of risk or the science of probability. It is rather a book that gives a practical view of risk management for any type of project or programme.

John Bartlett

About the author

John Bartlett manages a programme to support the management of projects and programmes throughout Europe, the Middle East and Africa for the Financial Solutions Division of NCR Ltd. Formerly, he spent two years as head of UK project management for DMR Consulting Group. Prior to this he enjoyed a long career at IBM UK Ltd, where he was engaged in programme and project management on behalf of clients in various business sectors, including government, insurance, banking and finance, retail, automotive and engineering. He was latterly involved in the management of IBM's Year 2000 Programme in Europe, and formed part of the programme executive team.

He is a Fellow of the Association for Project Management (FAPM) and an APM certificated practitioner of project management. He is also a Fellow of the Royal Society for Arts, Manufactures and Commerce. His book, *Management of Programme Risk*, which he edited and co-authored with David La Bouchardière, was published for CCTA by HMSO in 1995. His book, *Managing Programmes of Business Change*, first published in 1998 by Project Manager Today Publications, is now in its third edition. He has also published several project management papers and addressed conferences on programme and project management subjects. He also has a strong interest in music and the arts, and has published two reference books on decorative ceramics.

Using this book

This book will be of particular interest to project managers, middle and executive management, consultants, trainers and support staff who either need to practise or need to know about risk management It is not constrained by industry, and is applicable both to the public and private sectors.

It is arranged as follows:

Chapter 1 introduces the topic and sets out the applicability of risk management to business, projects and programmes.

Chapter 2 deals with the identification of risk and how to express it, so that it is unambiguous to others. It also tackles the differences between risks and issues and shows what can go wrong within each project phase.

Chapter 3 deals with the evaluation of risk, once identified, and introduces the concepts of probability and impact and how to put a value on risk.

Chapter 4 deals with the containment of risk through contingency plans and mitigation actions.

Chapter 5 focuses on the recording of risk, using both paper-based and software applications. It shows a suggested template for a risk register and risk log.

Chapter 6 focuses on risk analysis and risk reporting, and examines different ways of modelling risk and reporting it. There are several examples of charts that can be produced for different situations.

Chapter 7 covers the management and control of risk. It examines the various risk roles.

Chapter 8 summarises the key messages within the book.

A **Bibliography** contains books, journals and conference papers on risk, and provides information for further study. Obscure or difficult to obtain seminar and conference papers have been omitted. The UK Association for Project Management may be able to assist with finding papers published in its *Project* magazine, the *International Journal of Project Management* and the proceedings of the biennial *World Congress on Project Management*. Likewise, the US-based Project Management Institute (PMI) with its *Project Management Journal* for papers or its *Information Source Guide* for books.

A **Glossary** shows common risk management terms together with the chapters in which they appear.

Contents

Chapter 1

Introduction

THINKING ABOUT RISK

There is risk in everything we do. Crossing a busy road, bungee jumping, white-water rafting, making an investment decision and building a house are actions and activities which all contain risk. A participant in any of these is likely to weigh up the risks before taking part.

The nature of the risk assessment, of course, will vary greatly and will depend on the activity and the value the participant places on it with respect to personal risk. For example, crossing a busy road might be perceived by a young, street-wise city dweller to be such a mundane action that it requires only a cursory, almost subconscious thought before embarking on it. To an elderly country dweller, however, the same action might merit considerably greater thought. Yet, whereas it is possible to make such generalised statements regarding these two stereotypes, it is by no means certain that they will apply in every occurrence. Extenuating circumstances could cause the elderly country dweller to make no assessment of risk before crossing the road and vice versa.

What is more certain, though, is that none of these stereotypes is likely to undertake a written risk assessment before carrying out the action. This is more likely in activities such as making an investment decision or building a house, but again, it depends on how risk averse the participant is. Our perception is that few of our daily actions merit a formal risk management approach. We tend to balance monetary value against time and personal safety in arriving at the degree of risk we should take.

We are likely to identify with the newspaper headline 'Elderly man injured crossing road' in terms of how the accident could have occurred, since we tend to take a view that elderly people are more vulnerable in this situation. The headline 'City student injured crossing road' might cause us to search harder for causes, since we instinctively expect this situation to be a rarer event.

The moral here is that generalisation is fine as a starting point, though it rarely yields the best risk assessment. We need to apply greater depth to thinking about risk; but this does not mean it has to be a laboured activity.

Talking about risk to a colleague from the Far East recently, I was intrigued to discover that the Chinese word for 'risk' was appropriately 'wei ji', meaning 'danger opportunity'.

The juxtaposition of both the positive and negative aspects of risk seemed to me to make perfect sense. However, many projects tend to focus only on the negative aspect, whereas the business case for bothering with risk at all must surely focus on the positive aspect. I am convinced that good risk management is the key to many of the ills contemporary projects complain of: cost overruns, schedule conflicts, scope creep and resource shortages.

A question I like to ask project managers is 'How much time do you spend on risk management in your projects?'. The answer is rarely 'once a week', never 'daily', sometimes 'once a month' and often 'once a quarter'. The answer varies, though, according to the type of project. For IT related and general business projects the above is usually the norm. For safety critical engineering projects, I would hope that the answer would be different and that more attention would be given to risk management. Even so, I often hear that risk management is deficient in many examples of critical projects.

It is possible, of course, to manage a project without any form of risk management, but this itself carries a degree of risk. There will always be situations that could have been handled more efficiently or cost effectively had risk management techniques been employed. Risk management is often a trade-off between that which is essential to be achieved and that which is not. In other words, how assured do you want to be of a project's outcome?

My view is that a project manager should be thinking about risk on a daily basis – not necessarily formally, but at least informally. If weekly status reports are not showing differences in the risk register then insufficient attention is being given to risk management.

The old saying among project managers 'How do projects become late?' answered by 'One day at a time' has a worrying ring of truth. It is often the incremental 'creep' of projects in terms of scope, timescale and earned value that give credence to this saying. The only way we can tackle this problem is by practising risk management techniques, and on a daily basis. It does not mean that the project manager should be constructing risk analysis charts every day. It means that he or she should be applying thought in a risk-oriented way, and developing 'risk thinking teams' – but more of this later.

Some attempt to simplify what is, in fact, a complex subject, is sometimes made by prescribing templates. Indeed, I have often been asked for a 'starter set of risks' for a particular type of project, as if all conform to a level of predictability. The very notion that risk management is an exact science and so is able to be prescribed by templates is a much held fallacy.

The danger of prescription is that it can lead the project manager into a false sense of security – ie, for very little effort the project manager can feel he or she has produced a viable risk plan. Risk management does require particular effort, however, and should not be dismissed as a trivial exercise. Prescription can also stifle creativity, preventing project managers from giving deep thought to the real risks in a project. Templates can only test generalised and historically identified risks. They cannot test the specific combinations of objectives and activities that will be unique to the project. Good risk management is not prescriptive, but it should, of course, be able to draw on previous experience. There will be plenty of projects where a checklist of previous experience is a particularly useful starting point.

THE RISK-ISSUE-CHANGE PATHWAY

I find project managers are almost universally good at knowing that when an issue has occurred something has to be done to resolve it. They may not know what has to be done, but they certainly know that a process needs to be invoked. The issue is recorded and reported at Status Meetings, where it is probably discussed. Such issues, or problems as some prefer to call them, will demand time and, therefore, cost expenditure in order to resolve them. If a project change has to be raised in order to resolve an issue then this could bring an even greater cost. Also, there are often further risks associated with making a change and resolving an issue.

When a project is completed, the project close-out meeting invariably debates the issues that occurred during the life of the project. How much more efficient it might have been if many of the issues could have been foreseen as risks, and tackled as such! The cost of impact could have been saved. The 'fire-fighting' and running around trying to solve something urgently could have been avoided. There would have been no unplanned disruption to tasks, and the possibility of follow-on risks through resolving the issues could also have been avoided.

Surprisingly, though, few people make the connection between risks and issues. Today's risks are tomorrow's issues. Yet, if it is more efficient to deal with risks than issues, why do so few people think along these lines?

I believe it is partly a difficulty in differentiating between risks and issues (the next chapter deals with this) and partly a lack of precision that causes people to ignore the risks. It is easy to identify an issue, because it is here and present. A risk may impact at any time in the future – who can be precise about that? It is a difficult business case to persuade management to release money and resources to tackle a risk on such an expectation.

Yet experience shows that those who are able to 'bet the project' and spend money tackling risks benefit significantly.

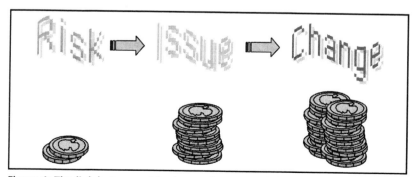

Figure 1: The link between risks, issues,changes and the relative cost of dealing with each

Many projects set aside an amount for risk in the original project business case. This might be a standard percentage or, infrequently, a figure derived from calculating an initial risk exposure. I find it strange, though, that having set aside this amount, managers are often reluctant to spend it on identifying and tackling risks. It is as if the money set aside in the name of risk is really for resolving issues, ie, when risks impact. This reverse logic is symptomatic of a focus on issues and a lack of risk-thinking which many project teams display.

Risks, issues and changes are often termed project exceptions, in that they are exceptional events (or ought to be) during a project's life-span. As project exceptions they have one thing in common – actions. Each needs one or more actions to tackle it. It is useful to know this since, as actions occur elsewhere in the cycle of project control, it is possible to be consistent about their presentation. Thus, actions from a project status meeting can be recorded in a similar way to actions from project exceptions. Ideally, actions should appear as tasks on the project plan, since the performance of actions requires time and effort, as does any other project activity. This provides a valuable management link between the plan and project exceptions. These latter should not be thought of as separate entities, though many tend to manage them as such. *(More on managing actions may be found in the chapter 'Mitigating risk').*

Understanding the risk-issue-change pathway is vital for developing a risk-thinking attitude. Occasionally, though, this can be abused. It is easy to fill a risk register with risks and pay lip-service to a process, so that when an impact occurs, a claim could be made that it was not the project manager's fault because the risk was recorded and reported. A true risk-thinking attitude is about taking mental ownership of the risks and an active desire to ensure that they don't impact as issues. This can be measured, of course, though I have yet to see a contract specify 'no more than 10 risks to impact as issues'! What is specified is the bottom line. Project managers are frequently measured on budget, time and quality, and good risk management has the ability to influence these outcomes significantly.

RISK MANAGEMENT APPLICABILITY

When and where to apply risk management is a question frequently asked. If you accept my view that it should be thought about at least daily, then the identification and assessment of risk is an ongoing activity right across a project or programme's life-span. There are, however, specific points in a life-span when risk management is particularly relevant. Figure 2 shows some typical risk management activities across project phases.

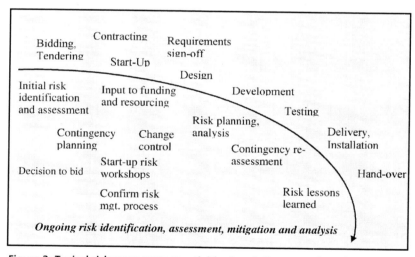

Figure 2: Typical risk management activities in relation to project phases

Pre-contract stage

Risk management plays an essential role well before a project gets under way. At the bidding or tendering stage it is important to identify and assess risks before proceeding to contract. The allocation of funding and resources should always be based on a formal risk assessment. Companies tend to have different ways of doing this, depending on their business requirements. Some use software questionnaires that produce weighted assessments of risk according to how questions are answered. Others open formal risk registers at this stage, so that risks identified can be seamlessly transferred into project execution.

Less widespread is any formal calculation of risk reserves for contingencies. Many companies will decide on a percentage of the total project cost for risk, eg, 5% or 10%. For very little effort, however, it is possible to calculate a proper risk exposure. The margin of error will be much less than 'finger in the air' guesswork and both the project team and the financiers will gain a degree of assurance through knowing that it is calculated from gathered data rather than guesswork. *(Details of risk exposure calculation may be found in the chapter 'Analysing and reporting risk').*

Establishing contingencies and contingency reserves at the pre-contract stage is important because they have a significant effect on project funding. I suspect most businesses would rather know at this stage not only the cost of a project in terms of resources over time but also its risk exposure. The former plus the latter equals the total potential cost of the undertaking. Any subsequent changes might be extra, of course.

Project start-up

Essential activities at project start-up are the establishment of a formal risk management process, to which all parties agree to subscribe, plus a start-up risk workshop. This latter activity re-checks the validity of the risks transferred from the pre-contract stage. Since all interested parties should be present (core team, suppliers, customers/users, etc.), it is a good opportunity to get the team into a risk-thinking frame of mind at an early phase of the project. *(See the chapter 'Identifying risk' for information about running a risk identification workshop).*

Once the project requirements have been formally signed off, the project should be under change control. Risk management has an important role to play during change control. Any project change being proposed should be assessed for risks. In fact, no change should be approved unless the impact of the change has been risk assessed. This should include re-visiting the current project risk register, in case the application of the change may alter probabilities, impacts and the validity and cost of actions and contingency plans.

As a project gets under way, risk planning and analysis need to become ongoing activities. The assignment of actions to contain risk and the monitoring of their progress and effectiveness is a fundamental part of risk planning. *(The chapter 'Mitigating risk' explores this activity in detail).*

The parallel activity of risk analysis is an important contributor to project decision-making, and something which many projects fail to undertake correctly. The project manager and sponsors need to be assured that the risk of moving forward is acceptable in terms of aspects such as cost, timescale and quality. *(Refer to the chapter 'Analysing and reporting risk' for details of this important activity).*

Tolerances may be defined to allow the project manager leeway in the management of risk. These are likely to be aligned to cost, time and quality. For example:

Functionality/Quality: zero tolerance

Time: + 1 week

Costs: +15% maximum, without further authorisation.

Project execution

The development phase of a project often presents a polarised view of risk. It can, on the one hand, re-assure project teams that the risks identified at project start-up are not so risky after all, or, on the other hand, reveal more risk if the deliverables being constructed are not as easy as originally believed. Of course, much depends on the nature of the project in this respect. Software development projects can be particularly problematic. Those using RAD techniques (Rapid Application Development), where phases are compressed, tend to reveal more risk during component construction. R&D (Research and Development) projects often commence with a high-risk perspective, owing to the unfamiliarity of the work to be undertaken, then reveal less risk as the project progresses and the team becomes more familiar with the product under development.

As an IT or product development project moves into its testing phase it is worth re-assessing the contingencies already identified for those risks whose impacts could have damaging consequences. Testing can reveal new information about a deliverable that can change the perspective of any associated risks. It can also generate new risks. It is, therefore, a good opportunity to re-visit the risk exposures of risks with contingencies. Testing may reveal that some contingencies will not be required (therefore, less cost) or that some contingencies may need to be increased (therefore, more cost).

Project completion

At project completion it is important to analyse the risks that were encountered and debate whether these were handled in the most appropriate and efficient way. Information learned from this activity can be used on future projects. When looking at lessons learned during a Project Completion Review, for example, some teams analyse only the issues encountered in the project. Few ask whether these issues could have been foreseen as risks. Yet merely examining this aspect can significantly help combat scope creep and margin erosion in future projects.

The programme view

At a programme level, risk management additionally includes the risk of benefits achievement. Otherwise, risk management plays a role similar to projects across a programme's phases:

- *During Programme Feasibility* it confirms the viability of the programme and provides the basis for judgements concerning the required investment and expected benefits.

- *During Programme Design* it supports the establishment of a firm foundation, building the confidence and assurance required to get the programme off to a good start.

- During the *Programme Execution* it provides a sound basis for ongoing management of the total programme risk exposure, and supports the requirements for problem resolution and programme changes.

- During *Benefits Realisation* it supports the successful transfer to the business of completed projects, the achievement of projected benefits and performance levels, the redeployment of resources and the feedback of 'lessons learned'.

A programme also has the benefits of scale, in that risk data can be rolled up from its constituent projects. Thus, risks identified in one project might also be applicable to another, so the programme risk manager is able to develop mitigation strategies suitable to both. Savings may be made in this way, and such economy of scale can be a significant benefit from taking a programme view of risk. For programmes that manage business change see *Managing Programmes of Business Change* for the role of risk in this specific area.

THE BUSINESS CASE FOR RISK MANAGEMENT

Managing risk takes time and costs money. Is it really worth doing on every project? Hindsight invariably shows that it is worthwhile. Quite apart from the side-effects of confidence building and team building that risk management can bring, the benefit to the bottom line is usually significant.

If you take the case of potential margin erosion, caused by things such as scope creep and re-work, risk management can reduce or even prevent it. Too many projects overrun their costs. The amount of overrun or a good proportion of it could have been a calculated risk exposure at project outset, and this risk exposure could have been mitigated.

For example, a project with a budget of £50,000 comes in at £75,000. If good risk management had been applied, the £25,000 overrun could have been identified as an initial risk exposure. Mitigation could have reduced this significantly. The £25,000 overrun need never have occurred.

I always cringe when I read about the massive overruns that some projects generate, especially those in the public sector. Was a risk exposure ever calculated? If so, were the risks mitigated? Surely, no one should embark on a project costing more than £100,000 without doing so?

Risk management is also a state of mind. A risk-thinking team brings benefits not only to a project but to the business as a whole. Such a team is confident, assured and will apply a creativity to work that might not otherwise develop. Risk management demands creativity in effecting the resolutions to potentially difficult problems. Avoidance, workarounds and contingencies need creative planning. These skills can be transferred to the normal business operation.

Chapter 2

Identifying and expressing risk

This is the bit project managers and project teams generally do not like doing! They know it has to be done, but it is often seen as a chore. This is probably why risk is sometimes only identified once during a project — at project outset, when all the team comes together for the first time. The challenge is: *how do we make risk identification and assessment interesting, important, and something that is practised at least weekly and thought about on a daily basis?*

Getting people to think about risk is, for many project teams, a cultural shift. Few project teams have been taught formally how to develop *risk thinking* approaches. There are many courses that teach the basics of risk management as a process, but few that concentrate on the thought processes for good risk management. In the introduction to this book I mention that we often subconsciously weigh up risks, such as when crossing the road. Businesses frequently require a more overt practice and many companies have dreamed up various ways to tackle this. Ubiquitous among these is the *risk checklist* – a way of formalising a judgmental process.

The risk checklist exists in many forms and attempts to give some assurance to the identification of risk. A series of questions or situations are typically presented, to which the project manager is required to respond. Responses are then weighted and an overall risk score is given. Depending on the score threshold the rating is either low, medium or high risk. Anything above low risk may trigger a specialist review or sign-off.

While this formalisation gets people to participate in a risk process, it is very mechanical, and such prescribed processes usually leave no room for creativity.

Risk questions or situations are good for setting the scene and can be thought provoking. However, as most projects are unique, there needs to be room to respond to the uniqueness of the project and the freedom to consider novel approaches to managing the risk within it.

A key starting point in tackling the attitudes to risk is to ensure that everyone knows how to identify and express risk in a foolproof way. Quite apart from promoting consistency, this enables everyone to overcome any fear factors in addressing risk and to ensure that the differences between a risk and an issue are fully understood.

EXPRESSING RISK

Many project teams seem to have a major difficulty in expressing risk. In other words, articulating the risk so that others can fully comprehend it. There is also widespread ignorance of the differences between a risk and an issue, such that many risks are often really issues and vice versa. If risks and issues are expressed correctly, however, there should be no doubt about which is which type.

Let's tackle the expression of risk first and then look at the differences between risks and issues.

In my role as auditor, I have often been presented with risk registers that look like this:

Risk	Probability	Impact	Mitigation
System testing	H	M	Check schedule
Testing resources	M	H	Assess resource requirement

This, I'm afraid, is often the norm for many projects. It is symptomatic of someone who has realised that risks need to be identified and logged and is paying lip service to a procedural requirement. The question is: 'Where's the risk?' It's a good question to ask, since what I have shown above are merely statements of project elements. They might be areas in which risks may reside, but they are not risks in themselves. In fact, they are quite good categories for risk investigation; but more of that later.

A response we might get to our question is:

1. *Systems testing may be late.*

2. *We may not have enough resources for system testing.*

That's better, the statements are looking more like risks, but we are missing some vital information. What's causing the risks?

Let's take the first risk. A typical response might be:

1. *Because of a need to add an extra module to the design there is a risk that systems testing my be late.*

Much better. But what's the effect?

Well, the project might overrun.

OK, so the risk is better expressed as:

1. *Because of a need to add an extra module to the design there is a risk that systems testing may be late, resulting in a delay to the project schedule.*

Perfect. Now we have cause, risk and effect, and in one sentence! No risk of ambiguity now!

Because of a need to add an extra module to the design	there is a risk that systems testing may be late	resulting in a delay to the project schedule
Cause	**Risk**	**Effect**

What about the other risk?

2. *Because of the holiday period there is a risk that insufficient resources will be available for systems, testing resulting in an extended testing period.*

Also much better!

For the risk register to have any value, though, we need to record more than just the statement of risk. A few control factors would be useful. *(The chapter 'Recording risk' shows how to record a risk, once identified.)*

Differences between risks and issues

Simplistically, an issue is a situation or an event that has occurred that will cause a detrimental impact to the project. Conversely, a risk is an event that has not yet occurred but may or may not occur in the future. The key question to ask is: 'Has the situation or event occurred, or not?'

However, like most things connected with projects, there are some grey areas. These usually concern project situations, rather than events. For example, a situation may exist that deals with an event that has not yet happened but is expected to happen at a point in the future. A common example is 'Stage 1 requirements have not been signed off by the business'. This sort of statement is often cited as an issue, but it is actually closer to one or more risks. The requirements have to be signed off before the project can continue into its design phase. Currently they have not been signed off, but they are expected to be signed off in the near future.

Business requirements sign-off ought to be a task on the project plan. It is only if the sign-off is already late or there is some concern about the sign-off that it becomes a worry to the project manager. If the task is late, you may wonder whether it would be more appropriate to raise it as an issue. The question to ask is: 'Is the project immediately impacted?' If the answer is 'yes' then it is an issue. If the answer is 'no', then it is a risk.

This situation could give rise to several risks, and could easily form part of the cause section of risk statements. For example:

Cause	Risk	Effect
Because Stage 1 requirements have not been signed off by the business, owing to unavailability of key board members,	there is a risk that the design phase will be held up,	resulting in a delay to the overall project schedule.
Because Stage 1 requirements have not been signed off by the business, owing to general indecision in the business,	there is a risk of several scope changes during the design and development phases,	resulting in a change to the the project target end-date and a significant increase in costs.

Table continues overleaf

Cause	Risk	Effect
Because Stage 1 requirements have not been signed off by the business, owing to a restructure of the business,	there is a risk that they may never be signed off,	resulting in cancellation of the current project.
Because Stage 1 requirements have not been signed off by the business in the current budgetary period,	there is a risk that the project will enter the next budgetary period,	resulting in a delay to the release of vital development funds.

If, as predicted by the penultimate item in the above list, the business decides not to sign off the requirements, that decision point (or event) is clearly an issue. Something has to be done about it immediately. The project might be saved by agreeing to a re-scope or it may have to be cancelled altogether.

There are many situations in projects where critical tasks are late, such as where a subcontractor should have delivered something and it has not arrived. It is tempting to call these issues, but, as we have seen above, they are more often risks. However, if work is prevented from continuing without whatever should have been delivered, the lateness is clearly an issue.

It is important that each project understands when a situation or event should be raised as an issue or risk. If the chosen project management methodology does not specify this, then the project office or project manager should ensure that the project exceptions procedure does. There *will* be grey areas, but it is hoped that the above examples will give some valuable guidance.

IDENTIFYING RISK

How do you identify risk? What is the best way of going about it?

Knowing how to express risk is a fundamental prelude to identifying it. The cause part of the risk statements we have examined points to a risk's origin. Risks will occur because of an event or situation. Therefore, we need to focus firstly on the things that can cause risk. These are widely known as the *risk drivers*.

Risk drivers are not risks in themselves, but the potential trigger points for risk. However, they need to be set in context. For example, a room used as a study might contain several risk drivers, but depending whether it was for use by an adult or by a child, the drivers would be of lesser or greater significance. Thus, power points, electrical cabling, paper shredder, sharp corners to a desk, letter opener and stapler would be greater risk drivers for a child.

In a business project it is possible to devise focus areas for the identification of risk. These might be sections of the project to which the team can easily relate. For example, product design, product development, product testing, project resources. These make useful categories within which risk may be analysed and reported. *(See also the chapter, 'Analysing and reporting risk'.)*

Within each of the focus areas are risk drivers. Thus, a useful prelude to identifying risk would be to construct a table of potential risk drivers against each focus area. Table 1 gives an idea of this for a software development project.

The focus areas and risk drivers mentioned above are internal to the project. Consideration also needs to be given to external focus areas, ie, areas outside the project that could cause concern. Table 2 gives some suggestions. Many projects suffer more from problems within the business or the marketplace rather than within the project. It is all too easy to forget the wider scope when immersed in the project detail.

Identification of the focus areas and risk drivers is best done in a

Focus area	Risk driver
Application design	Functional specification
Application coding	Version control Documentation Coding quality Resources
Integration testing	Test method Documentation
Systems testing	System performance Documentation
User acceptance	Test scripts User resources
Parallel running	Data version control Data consistency Data security
User training	Training method Training schedule Support

Table 1: Sample of focus areas and risk drivers for a software development project

workshop, where team members can reach a consensus, each contributing information from their particular areas of expertise. *(See the section in this chapter, 'Risk identification workshop'.)*

Once the focus areas and risk drivers have been identified, the next step is to ask 'what can go wrong' for each of the areas. I prefer to build up a risk concept map leading from the risk drivers to ever increasing degrees of impact. *(The chapter 'Analysing and reporting risk', 'Risk modelling' section, shows some examples.)* An important aspect of this map is that it shows causes and impacts. As we have seen from the section 'Expressing risk' in this chapter, the

Focus area	Risk driver
Business operations	User preparation User buy-in User requirements/expectations Quality standard Resources Security
Business organisation	Sponsorship Re-structuring Cost reductions Office rationalisation Globalisation Business culture
Legislation	Regulatory requirements/changes Health and safety Data protection Employment law
Marketplace	Consumers/customers Suppliers Prices Mergers and acquisitions
Climate	Fire, flood, storms
Political	War, strikes, protests, terrorism Changes in government

Table 2: Sample of external focus areas and risk drivers

risk statement needs to be linked to a cause or causes, resulting in an impact.

Various inputs to the risk identification process are useful, not least:
- the project plan

>if a plan has been constructed (ie, the project is not in pre–planning stage) then the tasks identified on the plan

are important inputs. If tasks are not yet available then a work breakdown structure could be just as useful.

- expertise

    gaining input from experts in particular areas of the project.

- precedence

    input from past project experience in the company – some companies have a knowledge database, capturing lessons learned from previous projects.

- industry knowledge

    input from similar projects in similar industries – some of this information may be proprietary, though increasingly much is now in the public domain via statutory requirements, professional bodies, etc.

- checklists

    best–practice guidance compiled from previous project experience. Checklists of open questions tend to be less cumbersome to use and more useful than checklists of closed questions.

- simulation tools

    many of the automated tools for identifying and assessing risk perform work on project planning software, running routines such as Monte Carlo simulation, which examines the possibility of tasks achieving their end dates. While this can be of great assistance, risk identification remains primarily a human activity.

These inputs can be assessed via:

- a risk identification workshop

    taking the opportunity to get the whole team focusing on risk in one session. While this is a useful forum for identifying risk, it is not practical to run this type of workshop every week. In order to embrace the continual process of identifying risk it will be important to seek regular input from other avenues.

- interviews

    obtaining information from team members and those external to the project.

- weekly status meetings

The risk identification workshop

The best way to identify risk is via a group session. Running a risk identification workshop is an excellent way of gaining team input, expertise and, importantly, buy-in to the risk management process. For this reason it is good to run such a workshop at project start-up and also, if appropriate, at client proposal stage. If it is run for the latter stage (and I suggest it should be the norm when creating client proposals of any substance) then the risks identified can be carried forward into the start-up workshop, should the contract be won. It is also good practice to run risk identification workshops at the completion of major milestones.

Scope and boundaries

The risk identification workshop can be run as a half-day, day or two-day session. Any less time than a half-day is likely to be unproductive; any more time than two days is likely to be too cumbersome for the participants.

It is important to set the boundaries before starting the workshop. My advice is to concentrate on identifying the risks rather than attempting to evaluate them as well. This keeps the workshop nicely contained. Identifying risks and assigning risk owners is as far as I prefer to go in one session, since it is the risk owners' job to ensure that evaluation is done, and this can be done later. Evaluating probability and impact in a large group can be time-consuming, involving extended debate, so a separate workshop is advisable. *(See 'Risk assessment workshop' in the chapter, 'Evaluating risk').* Also, in order to evaluate risks properly, additional input is usually required, and this is not always available from the expertise in the room. However, there will inevitably be some sort of discussion concerning probability and impact, which, of course, should be captured for later use.

Input material

A useful input to the workshop will be the project plan, if available. It is possible to prioritise the tasks on the plan and merely assess the most critical of these at the workshop. While this has value at subsequent risk identification workshops, I feel that it is beneficial at an initial workshop to be able to step back from the detailed tasks and assess the project environment as a whole through focus areas and risk drivers (see below).

Other useful material might be contracts, statements of work, the project work breakdown structure and organisation breakdown structure, lists of dependencies and assumptions, the current issue log and financial breakdowns, for example. If a Monte Carlo simulation has been run, then that output would be valuable for identifying duration and cost risks.

It is usually helpful to circulate project material in advance of the workshop.

Participants

Participants for the workshop should be the core project team plus other interested parties who are able to add value to the exercise. These should include all clients, subcontractors (working both externally and internally), sponsors, stakeholders, sales, procurement, finance, legal and HR (human resources), for example. It may not be possible to obtain a full team, but the more diverse the participants, the better the coverage will be. Having the sponsor(s) present will give encouragement to the team, even if present for only a short while.

An experienced facilitator will be required. This should not be the project manager. He or she will need the freedom to participate. A note-taker will be useful as much of the ensuing debate could be useful later when evaluating the risks. Someone will be needed to enter the risks into the risk register.

Agenda

The agenda can be fairly open within the overall time allowed. It is useful for the project manager to give an introduction and state the background to the project. Some of the participants may be meeting for the first time, so this is a great opportunity for team-building.

Deciding on the focus areas can be next on the agenda. The sub-projects, phases and divisions of the project can be a useful guide. It will probably be necessary to prioritise the focus areas in order to accommodate discussion within the time allowed for the workshop.

Next, the risk drivers can be identified. This can be accomplished to good effect by getting participants to write their suggestions, and the focus area to which they apply, on sticky notes, which can be arranged on a whiteboard. With the risk drivers suitably arranged, participants can then write suggested impacts. The impacts can be arranged as a flow extending from the risk drivers, similar to the risk concept map that I describe later in the chapter, 'Analysing and reporting risk'.

Now that causes and impacts have been identified, it only remains to extract the risks. Once this has been done, risk owners should be assigned. These should be assigned, where possible, during the workshop, so that you obtain consensus from the participants. Assigning them afterwards can be a protracted exercise.

The facilitator of the workshop should ensure that someone enters the risks and the names of the risk owners into a risk register. Output from the workshop should be a set of newly identified risks, ready for evaluation.

Agenda item	Responsibility
Welcome and project background	Project manager
The project in a business context	Project sponsor
Introduction to the workshop process	Facilitator
Identification of focus areas	All, lead by facilitator
Identification of risk drivers	All, lead by facilitator
Identification of impacts	All, lead by facilitator
Identification of risks	All, lead by facilitator
Assignment of risk owners	All, lead by project manager
Wrap-up and next steps	Project manager

Table 3: Suggested agenda for risk identification workshop

What could go wrong?

Some risk management books devote pages to the possible causes of risk. I prefer to highlight some of the more common situations that can cause risk during the lifespan of a project or programme, and let you decide how these relate to your own projects. Figure 3 shows some of the key influences that need to be kept in balance.

These key influences put the programme or project at risk. Some of these are internally manifested, others external to the

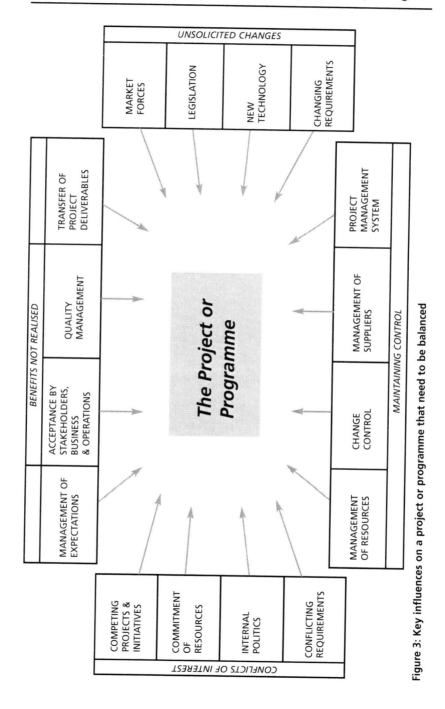

Figure 3: Key influences on a project or programme that need to be balanced

project and to the company. It is important to recognise these two environments — internal and external (ie, the near and the far). The former is relatively familiar and the latter often unfamiliar.

One of these groups of influences relates to control. The importance of maintaining control cannot be overstated. Results of not maintaining control can include excessive scope creep, unmanaged resources (both in-house and subcontractor) and a project management system that is not followed. Of course, project management is all about being in control, but it needs a strength of mind and purpose in order to effect it.

Change control is a particularly good example of where strong management is needed to ensure that the process is followed. So often, I've seen good processes in place that are not being applied — the spirit is willing but the flesh is weak!

The business itself is often its own worst enemy. Legacy processes, hidden agendas, ivory towers, internal politics and bureaucracy can all hinder a project's progress. Recognising these inhibitors is part of the way to solving the problem. Building and getting agreement to a sound project management system is another part. If the project needs to run at a faster pace than business-as-usual, then this must be negotiated up-front. For example, a need to obtain five signatures on a travel order may be fine for normal business operations, but for a fast-moving project it is clearly not.

Existing projects may well be competing for resources and also may be on a collision course with your own project. In large companies, few individuals know exactly what other initiatives are going on outside a particular business. A prime job of the project sponsor is to ensure that the project is not conflicting with other requirements.

The realisation of benefits may not be uppermost in the mind of a project manager when embroiled in the everyday operation of the project. However, particular project activities relate to the successful achievement of benefits, not least quality control. A good quality plan is an essential item, but many projects fail to produce one or examine the overall quality of what is being undertaken. Many concentrate just on testing, but testing is only one aspect of quality. The final proof is the acceptance of the deliverables by the client or end users. This will show whether quality has been given the correct attention.

Communication is another key requirement of project management. Benefits and quality are both influenced by good communication and the management of expectations. If these are managed well then the transfer of deliverables becomes relatively easy.

All the above are internal influences and relatively easy to manage. More difficult to manage are external events, such as market changes, government legislation or new technology. These can really stop a project in its tracks.

These and other influences are discussed further under the relevant project stage, below. I've used the standard, conceptual approach to these stages, viz:

(See also the section, 'Eight things to get right', in the chapter 'Managing risk'.)

Project start-up

Project start-up is one of the most fraught periods of a project's lifespan. It is usually accompanied by frenetic activity, often against the clock. Processes need to be established, plans need to be laid, suppliers need to be engaged and the team needs to be put in place. In short, there are many risks that can occur. However, it is also a period when many future issues may be avoided, since the start-up activity should be laying the foundations for the remaining phases of the project. It is, therefore, a period of opportunity. I liken it to decorating a room of a house. The majority of the work should be in the preparation. Over, say, a 5-day period, 3.5 days should be spent on preparing the surfaces and 1.5 days for pasting and wallpapering. Shortening the preparation phase runs the risk of problems at a later date.

The risks present in the project start-up phase are often self-imposed. An example is the temptation to start work before essential things are in place, for example supplier contracts or user requirements. The question often needing to be answered is 'How much work can be done (ie, how much risk can be taken?) without certain things in place?' This can only be answered properly by undertaking a risk assessment. Few people do anything as formal as this, though, and so run the risk of problems later on.

Failure to complete the start-up phase to a reasonable schedule can have a very demoralising effect on staff and can contribute to a high staff turnover at what is a critical phase in a project. Having project teams wound up and displaced can rapidly spell trouble.

Requirements sign-off

A key activity during start-up is to firm up the project requirements. It is the lynch pin for the whole project. Proceeding to work without a firm and agreed set of requirements is asking for trouble later on. 'Oh, but we always have change management', people often respond, to which I always reply: 'But how well do you enforce it?', I always reply. *(See 'Change management', below.)*

The risk of late requirements sign-off often appears on start-up risk registers. If there is any doubt about the firmness of requirements then it is usually a sign that the project is **not** ready to proceed to the design phase. The risk is more critical for fixed-price projects. If requirements and exclusions are not pinned down there will always be arguments later.

A key question to ask during start-up is whether the project is competing against other projects trying to do similar things? So-called 'collision course' projects are quite common in large companies where local initiatives are less understood across departments.

Top-down planning

Another important activity during start-up is the building of the project plan. This may be the ratification of earlier estimates (such as those submitted for a client proposal) or the construction of a new plan.

Any plan that has been handed down to the project manager (top-down planning), with fixed milestones and end dates must automatically be high risk. 'But all our projects are like this and I have no say in the key dates', is a common objection. For me, this is not project management. The true project manager is able to influence sponsors and stakeholders concerning the plan. It is fundamental to the role.

Getting resources and skills on board

Resource risks occurring during start-up are often related to the availability and commitment of resources, but cost and skills also feature. Establishing the right number of resources and skills seems never to be easy at start-up. If you commence work with resource deficiencies how long can you continue before difficulties occur? Resource planning should really occur during the pre-start-up phase, allowing time for a viable team to be recruited.

Resources assigned late in the project will inevitably increase costs, either directly through the cost of subcontractors, or indirectly through a possible decrease in productivity. A tendency towards undertaking tasks in parallel that were designed to be sequential is a symptom of late resource assignment. If work has to be compressed through the non-availability of resources then risk is transferred from project performance to the business operation, with the result that support and rectification costs multiply for the lower quality product delivered.

A key understanding is whether the project is competing against other projects and initiatives for particular resource. What position is the project against other things the company is doing? Is it the number one project for this year? The lower down the priority order, the less guarantee of commitment is the usual situation.

Contract sign-off

Like requirements, contract sign-off often features in the risk registers of projects during the start-up phase. The danger of proceeding with work without signed contracts needs to be understood. Each company will have different practices and requirements. It usually becomes more difficult to sign contracts once work has commenced. Negotiation powers are often reduced.

Contracts need to be examined carefully to ensure that they place individual risks with the party most able to effect its management – if risks are forced on inappropriate parties trouble is almost inevitable, and in many countries may be open to legal challenge under 'Unfair Contract Terms' legislation. Letters of intent are often seen as a way to expedite a project while the contract is awaiting sign-off by one party or the other – these can be commercially extremely dangerous and, within the confines of this text, the advice is that they should not be used.

Design

The design phase of a project is usually the period when the project team is presented with the reality of the undertaking. As requirements are translated into design, so the potential for risk increases. Probability is likely to reduce but the potential impacts of any risks not eliminated may rise dramatically.

Design specifications sign-off

Both requirements sign-off and design sign-off are critical activities at the start-up and design phases respectively. In a software development project this would be the sign-off of a functional specification. In a construction project this would equate to building specifications and drawings. The design phase is a good test for whether the requirements are firm. It is also a test for whether the requirements are feasible. If the requirement is for something totally new there will be no precedent for the work. Has it been done before? ... in the company? ... in the industry? These are relevant questions to ask when considering risk here.

In some projects there is an integrated research and development stage, such that design specifications have to be framed in terms of developing the technologies. This development stage needs to be planned, production managed, risk assessed and risk managed.

Resources and skills availability

The design phase should give a better indication of the requirement for particular skills and resources. As with the start-up phase, their availability could give rise to risk. Commitment of resources for the required period of time is often a cause for concern, as is the general availability in the marketplace of a particular skill. Compare the use of new oilfield technology offshore where no pool of uncommitted, competent operatives exists to date, to a standard house-building project, where a widespread pool of skilled resource is available.

Where in-house resources are not available, subcontracted resources may be an option. These require advance planning and cost approvals. Managing the cost of subcontracted resources effectively is no mean task.

Build

As work gets under way, the unfamiliar becomes the familiar, and many of the risks identified in earlier phases are lessened or cease to be relevant. Component production risks, for example, are closed out after their build is complete. This is not to say that the build phase is not without risk. New risks can be identified, many of which may test the resilience of the schedule and the quality systems.

Change management

Change management is one of those processes that looks great on paper but is often difficult to accomplish in practice. The danger is that acceptance of small changes outside the change control procedure contributes to scope creep. Much depends on the culture of the company. Some companies are able to enforce change control, while others have a more loose interpretation of changes and usually suffer as a result. Some projects undoubtedly have slack in the schedule in which to accommodate small changes, but if changes are accepted outside a formal process there is no ability to add up the knock-on effect of incremental change and the changes created in the overall picture of risk. For example, changing a value in a line of code in a software program may seem innocent enough, but its effect on dependent code could be significant.

Expectation management

Ensuring a match between requirements and expectation is an

important activity for any project. So many projects have foundered because the outcome did not meet customer expectations. The solutions may have been technically elegant, but it they are not what the end-users need or can use then they have clearly failed. Again, clarity and agreement as to what is excluded from the project scope should be established from the earliest stages of project initiation.

Contributing to risks of poor customer or user expectation are poor communications management and poor quality management. In order to reduce the surprise element to users of what is to be delivered, there needs to be regular communication and involvement. Prototyping is one of many opportunities for users to gain a 'hands-on' view of deliverables, and user involvement in the quality assurance processes is vital.

Key questions to ask are:

- What opportunities are planned for end-user communication and sign-off? Requirements? Design? Materials checks? Prototypes? Usability test? Acceptance test?

- How are end-users to be involved in the project? For reviews and feedback? For quality assurance? As testers?

- Do the project executors fully understand how the deliverable is to be used and exploited by the end-users?

Test

The testing of products, whether as a discrete phase or alongside development, is a typical breeding ground for risk. The predictability of outcomes is often difficult, such that a period set aside for testing is frequently over-run. This can have a knock-on effect on other projects waiting to use the test facilities.

If there is pressure to curtail testing, in order, for example, to meet a particular deadline, then the risk of post-implementation failure must be greater. Also, additional costs may be expended in support.

Resources and skills availability

Resources for testing always seem to be difficult to obtain. Planning their availability in advance may give some assurance, but there are often problems marshalling them on the actual dates required. The administrative workload in scheduling resources to test plans is often underestimated. Also, in the event of a problem, it may be difficult to obtain specialist resources for rectification purposes.

Test environment

The availability of specialist test environments and tools is often a cause for concern. Has the test environment itself been tested, so that when it needs to be used on an appointed day everything works?

Is the team clear on what types of testing are required? For example, unit (component) testing, regression testing, stress testing, volume testing, integration testing, acceptance testing, usability testing.

Test results

Predicting the outcome of tests is itself often high risk. In a software development project that has a discrete testing phase, errors in the code will be logged daily but decisions about whether to continue testing may not be taken until the end of each week. A two-week acceptance test, therefore, could easily last six weeks.

In a product development project much will depend on the nature of the tests being carried out. Stress testing of engineered components, for example, is more likely to be predictable in outcome than usability testing, which is notorious for revealing the unexpected.

Hand-over

Hand-over can be formal or informal, depending on the nature of the project. Formal hand-overs often require certificates of acceptance, but even informal hand-overs need some form of recognition of the transition from project to business-as-usual. It is an area subject to potential confusion between project team and client, particularly concerning the boundary of transition from, say, project support to operational support.

User preparedness

The readiness of the user organisation to receive the deliverables is often a focus for risk. If expectations have been set regularly throughout the project then the risk of non-acceptance is lessened. A question to ask is: 'How prepared is the user organisation in terms of training, support, facilities, business processes and user documentation, for the change being delivered?'

Where the deliverable is a physical product, unscheduled costs and risks may be incurred by the receiving organisation with the unexpected delivery of the product (manning, storage, insurance, for example), for which the organisation may seek reimbursement.

Benefits

Hand-over should include the provision for monitoring the effectiveness of the changes implemented. In a programme this is the role of the business change manager, but for a stand-alone project the role needs to be specified, probably within the user community. The risk of non-achievement of benefits depends on many factors, not least user take-up. Benefits will accrue over time, but unless a measurement process is in place the original project sponsors will not see how their investment has been realised.

For certain projects, the benefit achievement can only be delivered by the integrated delivery of a programme (eg, a new warehouse facility which integrates building, IT systems, staff recruitment and training projects).

Chapter 3

Evaluating risk

Once a risk has been identified it needs to be evaluated for its likelihood of occurrence and its possible impact. This is where the real science of risk management comes into play.

In order to evaluate a risk you need good data. In particular, you need to know about:

- the environment in which the risk has occurred

- the environment it may impact on

- whether the risk has occurred before:

    - in your project

    - in your business

    - in your industry

and how it was mitigated and the effect of that mitigation.

At a general level you will need basic data regarding your project, such as the overall cost of the project in terms of people and resources, and the approximate daily value of keeping the project going. This is so that any impact that represents a delay to the project can be adequately calculated.

Less easy to calculate are any indirect costs, such as:

- lost sales
- lost opportunities
- loss of market position and/or share
- liquidated damages payable to a client.

Notwithstanding this, evaluation is very much a perception, and being a perception it is subject to a large margin of error.

This is why it is always helpful to record comments concerning the evaluation of any risk. The perception at the time the risk was evaluated may differ from later evaluations. By recording comments at the time of evaluation, later assessors can see why a risk was rated as a particular probability or impact. If conditions have changed then a new rating can be applied.

The chapter, 'Recording risk', shows the detailed fields in the evaluation layer of a standard risk register. You may find it helpful to review this with the text below.

ASSIGNING RISK OWNERS

Each risk on the risk register needs to have ownership. This ensures that it is not just something recorded, but that someone is actively working to ensure that it is evaluated, re-evaluated and mitigated.

Not many projects seem to bother with assigning owners for individual risks. I think this is poor practice. Making someone accountable for a risk ensures that it is not left unattended and that it has a chance of being properly evaluated. Assigning an owner also directs responsibility to the person most skilled to evaluate the risk. Leaving this to the person who raised the risk is not necessarily effective, unless the raiser happens to be the ideal candidate for risk owner. It is not always easy to assign a risk owner, but should at least be attempted. In my experience, risks without risk owners are often the ones that are left without actions.

The project manager would assign a risk owner once a risk has been identified. The risk owner should be someone who has some affinity with the risk. It is often the person who raised the risk, but not exclusively. In this case, that person has a vested interest in ensuring that the risk is suitably dealt with. A risk owner may own more than one risk. This is particularly useful where risks are related or interdependent.

(The role of the risk owner is described in the section, 'Risk roles', in the chapter 'Managing risk'.)

ESTIMATING PROBABILITY AND IMPACT

Evaluation is primarily concerned with assessing the probability of the risk occurring and its impact on the project. These are the elements that are highly subjective. Even if there is data to support a previous occurrence in a similar situation on a similar project, the calculation of probability can only be a rough estimate. Because of this, many project teams assess probability and impact merely as high, medium or low. I feel this is so vague and non-committal that it is really not worth doing. Even with the margin of error I prefer to use a much finer granularity, and so recommend the use of percentages.

(In the chapter, 'Analysing and reporting risk', I show how probability and impact can be used to monitor risk and to report it.)

Probability

For rating probability, I suggest using a percentage. This is much better than using high, medium and low as ratings. In percentage terms, 'high' would equate to a figure of anything from between 67% and 99%, which leaves a considerable margin of error. A probability of 70% ought to be quite different from that of 90%; and to rate them both as merely 'high' and, therefore, treating them as similar in probability terms, is not good practice.

You will notice that I refrained from using 100% as a probability. This is because I view a risk with a 100% likelihood as an event that is definitely going to take place, ie, as an issue and not as a risk. Consider, for example, a risk of government legislation being passed that would impact on your project. There is no doubt that a risk should be raised in this case. However, if the legislation has already been passed, but will not come into effect until a fixed date in the future, that is not a risk but an issue. There is no risk that the legislation will not happen, so the project will have to take immediate action to avert the impact. (*See also 'Differences between risks and issues', in the chapter 'Identifying and expressing risk'.*)

What equates to high, medium and low in terms of probability is subject to debate. Some risk managers would say that anything above a 40% probability is high risk and deserves a priority response. Some would argue that probabilities above 50% should be treated as certainties in terms of action response. Whatever view you might favour, it is important that everyone in the team understands the meaning of the probability thresholds you wish to set.

Attempting to estimate a probability between 1% and 99% can be quite daunting for those not used to having to evaluate against such a large range. My recommendation is not to be too concerned about the initial evaluation of probability, since, over time, as more people see the risk and discuss it and more data becomes available, the percentage can be refined. Probability will come under closer scrutiny when people start to consider seriously the cost of impact.

I remember, when assessing the overall risk impact for my company of the implementation of the Euro currency, that the team's initial estimate of impact was higher than the final estimate. What was driving this estimate was probability. It was being used in a multiplier to estimate the contingency fund in case problems arose on E-day. Once people started to question the accuracy of the probability estimate new data was sought and it was refined accordingly. In this case, the probability decreased – not just as a result of new data but also as a result of the work being done to mitigate the risks.

Many probability estimates reflect an unfamiliarity of work to be performed. As a project team begins to execute the work confidence usually builds and probability estimates decrease. Of course, this does not always happen!

Impact

For me, impact is mainly an expression of cost and is best assessed in monetary units. I know there are other ways in which it can be expressed, such as in terms of productivity. Ultimately, however, it leads to a cost – a cost that has a direct link to the project budget.

When assessing impact, I like to think of the repair cost of the damage caused. For some projects this is an obvious physical thing, such as a pipe burst. In business and IT projects, for example, it is often non-physical, and usually relates to time lost. In physical impacts a repair cost could also be a replacement cost, if the object cannot be repaired. In non-physical projects the repair cost could also be a contingency or workaround cost, if no more time could be squeezed from the schedule in order to make the repair.

This is basically how insurance companies work when underwriting risk. Sophisticated tables are used to calculate probabilities and an estimate to repair is made based on a replacement price with allowance for wear and tear in many cases. The level of sophistication needed for your project will be dictated by the nature of your project and your company standards.

Sometimes the cost of repair may relate to a more indirect cost, such as loss of life, loss of sales and revenue. These will be more difficult to estimate. Expressing impact as a repair cost is a good basic approach, however.

Additionally, I like to express the impact cost as a percentage of the project budget. This really puts a focus on the risk in relation to the project as a whole. A risk with an impact of 110% of project budget would certainly get some attention at the weekly project status meeting!

Table 4 gives an example of some of the types of impact against types of repair cost. Using 'time delay' as an example, the table shows that the repair cost relates to the cost of retaining all or part of the project team for an additional period. This is the most common form of impact repair. It could, for example, arise from a sub-team over-running, thus holding up the next stage of work. In this case, the repair cost might be 3 resources at £1500 per week for 3 additional weeks, being a total of £4,500. If the probability of the impact occurring is set at 60%, then the risk exposure is £2,700 (£4,500 x 60%).

Some impacts could be so damaging to a project that a contingency plan needs to be put in place. When evaluating impacts it is always worth considering their criticality. 'Could the project survive if a particular risk impacted?' is a question worth asking of every risk. If the answer is no, then a contingency plan might need to be drawn up. *(Contingency plans are discussed in the chapter 'Mitigating risk'.)*

CALCULATING THE RISK EXPOSURE

For me, one of the most important aspects of risk evaluation is the risk exposure. Any senior manager requesting base information about a project needs to know at least three figures: (i) the project cost; (ii) the project benefit; (iii) the risk exposure.

Compare the following three projects:

Project	Cost	Benefit	Risk exposure
1. Replace sales order system	£0.5m	£3m savings	£0.2m
2. New product offering	£0.5m	£6m revenue, year 1	£1.8m
3. New accounting system	£3m	£12m savings	£5m

Type of impact	Typical reason	Type of repair cost
Time delay	Incorrect estimates of workload; unexpected additional work	The cost of retaining all or part of the project team for the required repair time
Contingency	Impact would be devastating to the project and the likelihood of impact would be too high to risk any damage occurring	The cost of supplying or reserving something in case a risk impacts. Money set aside in case of impact
Resource/skill shortage	Holidays, sickness, skill deficiency	The cost of hiring an additional resource for a required period
Benefits impact	Likelihood that certain benefits may not be met	The cost of re-specifying the existing requirements, plus any compensation to a client for benefits not met
Marketing impact	Risk that user communities do not fully understand the deliverables	The cost of additional external or internal marketing and end-user support
Travel impact	The need for travelling may have been underestimated	The cost of additional travel and associated accommodation
Training/support impact	Feelings that training may not be adequate	The cost of specifying and supplying additional training or support

Table 4: **Example of types of repair cost to risk impacts**

Without the risk exposure information, project three looks attractive. With the risk exposure, however, it looks much less attractive. As a decision-making tool, risk exposure is a vital component. Even though there may be a large margin of error in its calculation, risk exposure is a powerful criterion when used in comparing projects.

In its simplest form, risk exposure (RE) is calculated by multiplying the impact repair cost (IRC) by the probability of occurrence (P). Thus, £IRC x P% = £RE. The risk exposures for each risk are added to form a total for the whole project.

The overall risk exposure is, of course, reduced by the effect of mitigating actions. So, in calculating the risk exposure for a project at, say, pre-contract stage, it is logical to add in the effect of potential actions (reduction in probability and reduction in impact). If, for example, a project RE is calculated to be £120,000, but feasible actions can be estimated to reduce that to £25,000, then the risk exposure becomes £25,000. The cost of actions needs to be added, however. If the cost of the actions is £5,000 then the total risk exposure is, therefore, £30,000. The total £RE can be added to the project budget.

Some project managers like to apply weightings to particular types of impact or priority of risk. These can increase or reduce the risk exposure. However the final result is calculated, it is important to remember that the result is only a guideline, a comfort factor and, at best, a form of comparison. It is certainly better than nothing and, when project experience is fed back into the equation, it can improve in accuracy year on year.

Companies practising corporate management of change through strategically aligned programmes would probably want to set a company standard for the calculation of risk exposure. Such an accounting convention would enable the company to roll up the risk exposures of programmes and their constituent projects in order to plan its annual budgets for corporate change.

SETTING RISK PRIORITIES

Having identified a list of risks it is helpful to know which ones to tackle first. Severity of impact is probably the best criterion to help decide, though other factors need to be considered as well.

The urgency of a risk is one such factor. Any impact that is imminent would need to be dealt with urgently, depending on the severity of its impact. Often there are critical windows for actions, so while a risk impact may be some time off, the opportunity to manage it effectively might be imminent.

You may find it useful to construct a matrix of probability against impact so that you can see more easily which risks to prioritise for assigning actions. *(See the section, 'Examples of risk charts', in the chapter, 'Analysing and reporting risk', for an example).*

Priorities can be set in several ways. High, medium or low is a common three-fold representation. Some projects prefer to use priority numbers – anything from priority 1 and 2 up to 6. It is important to ensure that everyone understands what the priorities mean. High, medium, low or 1, 2, 3 need to be qualified. I prefer to keep the levels of priority to a minimum and find that two levels are usually adequate. Thus:

Priority 1	Risks that will seriously damage the project if they impact
Priority 2	Risks that will have a contained effect on the project but will not seriously damage it

This rating caters for both urgency and severity. It is simple and easy to remember. However, I recognise that for certain technical projects being managed to close tolerances a finer granularity is desirable.

Don't be tempted to ignore risks that are low in impact cost. Even little impacts if they occur excessively frequently become wearing, which damages team morale and increases the possibility of more severe errors.

THE RISK ASSESSMENT WORKSHOP

In large projects it may be desirable to hold a group session to determine the evaluation of risks identified in a previous session. More accurate evaluations can usually be obtained through such a session, since participants are dedicating themselves to a single aim. A risk assessment workshop is valuable for risks requiring input from several parties, where evaluation can be debated and argued. This is often held following a risk identification workshop *(Chapter 2)* and follows a similar format. Risk owners will have a key role to play in the workshop, since they will have gathered base material for discussion concerning the risks they own.

Scope and boundaries

The risk assessment workshop can be run as a half-day, day or two-day session. Any less time than half a day is likely to be unproductive. Any more time than two days is likely to be too cumbersome for the participants. It is important to set the boundaries before starting the workshop. The workshop performs both the activities of evaluation and mitigation. The output of the workshop, therefore, would be a set of fully evaluated risks plus suggestions and actions for mitigating them, including ownership of those actions.

On a two-day workshop it can be useful to arrange for the overnight production of the formal documentation of the results of the first day's work.

Participants

Participants for the workshop should be the core project team plus other interested parties who are able to contribute. This should include the client, as applicable, subcontractors (working both externally and internally), sponsors, stakeholders, sales, procurement, finance, legal and HR (human resources), for example. It may not be possible to obtain a full team, but the more diverse the participants are the better the coverage will be.

An experienced facilitator will be required. This should not be the project manager. He or she will need the freedom to participate. A note-taker will be useful, as much of the ensuing debate could be useful later when evaluating the risks. Someone will be needed to enter the risks into the risk register.

Particular experts will need to be identified before the workshop if their input is needed for evaluation and mitigation. These may well be people from outside of the core team.

Agenda

The agenda can be fairly open within the overall time allowed. It is useful for the project manager to give an introduction on the current state of the project prior to the introduction of the workshop process by the facilitator.

The current risk register should be distributed to all attendees prior to the workshop. The first step is to undertake an initial prioritisation of the risks in the risk register. This can only be a quick assessment, since in order to undertake prioritisation fully one needs to know the probabilities and impacts, which will only be done later in the workshop. This initial priority is so that the risks can be evaluated in order of importance. If the number of risks to evaluate is small then they do not need to be broken down further. If the number is large then it is useful to break down the risks into sub-groupings, either by type, by focus area or by risk owner.

The next step is to decide on the probability of occurrence for each of the risks in each category, starting with the highest priority. Then the cost of impacts can be evaluated, followed by the re-prioritisation of the risks.

Starting with the highest priority risks, suggestions for

Agenda item	Responsibility
1. Welcome and project status	Project manager
2. Introduction to the workshop process	Facilitator
3. Quick prioritisation of risks in the risk register	All, led by facilitator
4. Identification of risk probabilities for high priority risks	All, led by risk owners
5. Identification of impact costs for high priority risks	All, led by risk owners
6. Calculation of risk exposures	All, led by facilitator
7. Re-prioritisation of risks	All, led by project manager
8. Identification of mitigation actions for high priority risks	All, led by risk owners
9. Repeat 4-6 for the next order of priority	All, led by risk owners
10. Wrap-up and next steps	Project manager

Table 5: Suggested agenda for risk assessment workshop

mitigation actions may be taken next. The risk owners should lead this step ideally, identifying experts who can give input.

If time permits, risks in the next order of priority may be assessed.

The facilitator of the workshop should ensure that someone is able to update the risks in the risk register and that any issues identified are entered in the issues log.

Chapter 4

Mitigating risk

Clearly, the most important aspect of risk management is the mitigation of risks that have been identified. Yet, this is probably the least well done of all the risk management activities. Several things work against the adequate mitigation of risk.

Firstly, there is capacity. Risk mitigation is not usually an activity that can be done instantly. It requires concentrated thought.

Secondly, there is cost. There are usually costs associated with carrying out risk actions. The feasibility of these has to be weighed against the severity of the risk and the likelihood of occurrence.

Thirdly, there is the concept of probability. 'If we do nothing, will things really be as bad as we have evaluated?'

Fourthly, there is schedule. Identifying mitigating actions adds tasks and, therefore, time to the project schedule. This is usually not budgeted for at the outset of the project.

Fifthly, there is expertise. One person is unlikely to have the expertise required to mitigate all the risks. Input from various quarters will be necessary.

Sixthly, there is commitment needed to carry out the required actions. Commitment to risk actions should be as great as to the tasks on the project schedule, but many people will find themselves under time pressure and will not always be able to fulfil the actions.

Understanding the capacity, cost, probability, schedule, expertise and commitment of adequately mitigating risks is one of the first routes to successful risk management. This chapter attempts to show how mitigation can be carried out effectively.

DECIDING ACTIONS

Project managers are traditionally concerned with the three attributes of time, cost and quality.

In a project a risk impact usually means cost. It could also mean time and quality, of course, but even these attributes can often be translated into cost. Extending or losing time costs money and achieving quality cost money. You could argue that projects or programmes with an immovable end-date, such as calendar-related events, have 'time' as an end-point, but with few exceptions (the Year 2000 computing problem rectifications, being one) date-based events can be moved, though probably not without cost. The European Central Bank could have moved the start date for the introduction of the Euro currency, but the cost of doing so would have been significant.

In a programme, the impact end-points can be more subtle. Loss of business reputation can feature regularly, but again this can translate into lost revenue, therefore, 'cost'. A threat of litigation is another regular impact these days, and also translates into cost, often significantly so.

It is important to bear in mind the ultimate impact points when deciding actions for dealing with risk. These should steer your direction so that you take the most appropriate courses of action.

The people most suited to recommend actions are the risk owners. *(See 'Assigning risk owners' in the chapter, 'Evaluating risk'; and 'Risk roles' in the chapter, 'Managing risk'.)* Their expertise can ensure that the most appropriate actions are devised with the most appropriate people allocated to carry them out. Their recommendations, however, need to be set in the context of the project as a whole. The project manager, therefore, will need to approve any actions, as he or she is the budget holder.

Assuming the prerequisites of expressing and evaluating risk have been done, the first step is to decide what type of action is appropriate to mitigate the risk. 'Mitigate' means 'lessen in severity', but this is not always the most appropriate form of action. You might want to accept the risk, avoid it, or insure against it, for example, rather than reduce its impact or the chances of it occurring.

If you accept that the risk might occur, you might want to counter its impact by specifying a contingency plan. For example, a risk that an in-house test facility may not be available within a particular time period might be countered by reserving an off-site test facility. (See Action A0204 002 below.) The cost of cancelling a reservation if it is not eventually required is likely to be a small price to pay for having the assurance of a contingency.

Contingency plans are often specified in conjunction with mitigating actions. So, in the example above, we might wish to specify an action to reduce the risk of the in-house facility not being available, as action A0204 002 below.

Mitigating risk is time-consuming. There are no short cuts to

Action No.	Mitigation action	Action owner	Priority	Due date	Reduction in prob.%	Reduction in impact%	Cost £K	Action status
A0204 001	Make a reservation on an off-site test facility	EGH	1	01/05/02	0	50	3.5	02.05 Done
A0204 002	Check detailed schedule with in-house test facility manager and identify gaps	EGH	2	25/04/02	10	0		02.05 Gaps in test schedule but test ready date not yet certain

doing it well, so you need to be able to relate the effort required to the end result. So often, I have seen actions specified that would clearly have little or no effect on the risk, either in terms of reducing its impact or reducing its likelihood of occurrence. To me, such actions are a waste of effort. When deciding actions, it is important to specify only actions that will have a real effect on the risk. One way to check this is to estimate the amount of reduction in impact and/or probability that the action will achieve.

In the example above, the reduction in impact and probability has been estimated for each action if it is carried out successfully. Action A0204 001 would have no effect on reducing the percentage probability, which was originally estimated at 50%. This is because it is a contingency action, and contingency actions only have an effect on the impact. If the original estimate of impact was 10% of the total project cost, action A0204 001 would remove the threat of impact entirely. Contingency actions usually have costs associated with them, so the cost of undertaking the action has to be added to the risk exposure. In this example, the cost of undertaking the action is £3,500.

Conversely, action A0204 002 indicates that the risk owner believes 10% of the probability could be reduced by carrying out the action. So, once this action has been completed, the project manager would expect to reduce the overall probability of the risk occurring from 50% to 40%. Action A0204 002 indicates no effect on the impact. This is because the action is only to check the status of something and not to reduce the damage that might occur if it impacts.

Indicating the reduction in probability and impact helps to select which actions should take priority, ie, the ones that will have the most effect. It also shows whether additional actions are needed to reduce the impact or probability further. More importantly, it acts as an effective check on the validity of actions, and so, prevents time being wasted.

Some actions will be preparatory actions for larger, more effective actions. These are often actions that require someone to find out or check something, as we have seen in the example, A0204 002, above. They will consequently have no effect on impact or probability, but are nonetheless important. In the example above, A0204 002 could be considered a preparatory action for the first action, even though some reduction in probability is indicated, ie, *check the in-house testing schedule and if it is really not suitable then carry out the contingency plan.* The contingency plan effectively takes care of the risk impact, but it is a relatively expensive option. The project manager would probably prefer to mitigate the risk by other means. The second action does not reduce the risk sufficiently, however, so other actions would need to be specified.

Sometimes a risk bears such consequences that the aspect to which it relates becomes untenable. This means that an alternative solution is required so that the risk may be avoided. Avoiding risks in its simplest term means finding a work-around, but could easily mean a major change to a project's direction. It is fairly common in software, research and development, and similar innovatory projects, for the need to avoid risks.

Another method of dealing with risk is to insure against it. This is popular in the construction industry, where insurers are used to providing cover for particular types of construction risk. Insuring against a risk does not prevent it happening, but it does provide some compensation if it impacts. In many ways, it is like a contingency action. There is always a cost involved (the premium cost) and it relates to a project critical situation.

(See the chapter, 'Recording risk', for information on recording actions in the project risk register and the chapter, 'Managing risk', for information regarding the roles of the action owner and risk owner.)

Type of risk action	Description	Example
Contingency	Actions designed to avoid or reduce the impact of a risk.	1. Reserve additional hire time for heavy-duty digging equipment. 2. Take out insurance to cover the risk of damage.
Investigative	Actions that gather information or check the existence of something. These actions may or may not reduce the probability. They rarely reduce the impact, unless the investigation reveals, for example, that the impact would not be as severe as estimated.	Find out how many employees have 'xyz' software installed on their PCs.
Counter measure	Actions that directly counter a risk. These actions can reduce both the probability and the impact. They are often suggested following the result of an investigative action.	For a risk that some employees may not be aware of the new company health and safety guidelines, typical counter-measure actions could be to send out the new guidelines to all employees or train employees in the new guidelines.
Workaround	Actions designed to avoid a risk by working around it.These actions may reduce both the probability and impact. They can also cause project changes. They are frequently suggested following the result of an investigative action.	1. Change the approach to capturing 'abc' data from the help desk. 2. Do not implement the new release of software until the 'xyz' feature has been stabilised.

Table 6: Summary of the more common types of risk actions

Managing assumptions

Most projects proceed on a basis of assumptions. Requirements and scope, in particular, are usually full of assumptions. Decisions during the course of a project are made against this background of assumptions, and the hope is that the project assumptions can eventually be turned into actualities, so that more assured decisions can be made.

The problem for risk management is that, in mitigating risk, actions are often being decided against assumptions. So a validation needs to be made against the data being presented before an action is agreed. For example, is the data reliable? Where did it come from? Who agreed it? What precedent is there for making the assumption?

Many assumptions made pre-contract are able to be ratified post-contract. For a fixed price contract this is especially desirable. Thus, for example, an assumption that a product will be developed and rolled out to 200 branch offices should be ratified in the statement of requirement. If it is not, and many projects proceed on the basis of unratified assumptions, then there is a risk that the assumption is incorrect. In many cases, the change management process will support such changes to the project requirements, but small assumptions that tend to compound other assumptions are often not captured by this process.

Assumptions need to be regularly tested for validity. Unless assumptions are formally logged they could be interpreted as fact by anyone needing to use them. For example, a business analyst may make an assumption about a user requirement. A software designer may take that assumption and build it into a system design. A software programmer may use that assumption to write code. A test writer may use it to design a test program. The test designer could interpret the assumption as fact, since it has been through many hands before it reaches him or her.

The risk of mitigating actions being invalidated through incorrect assumptions has to be recognised as a distinct possibility. Risk owners, in particular, need to be aware of changes occurring to assumptions used to mitigate the risks they own.

MANAGING ACTIONS

Day-to-day administrative management of actions is often vested in the project office. This would comprise checking due dates and chasing action owners for responses, recording progress and ensuring that the status of risks is generally maintained. If web-enabled interactive software is installed, then action owners and risk owners should be able to receive reminder emails of approaching and overdue action dates. Reports of overdue dates may be produced for the project manager, together with analyses of impacts to the project resulting from any overdue actions.

'At what point is a risk considered fully mitigated?' 'When do you close a risk?' 'What do you do if a risk impacts?' These are commonly asked questions about managing actions.

Some risks are never closed, and remain on the risk register throughout a project's life. This is usually because an element of risk always remains. Mitigating actions may have reduced the risk to the lowest level of severity, but cannot entirely eradicate it. Some risks may be closed if actions are able to eliminate it. Some risks are closed because they are no longer relevant (for example, design delay risks can be closed out at the completion of a design phase). Some risks may be closed because they have impacted, so need to be transferred to the issues register. If all your risks, issues and changes are maintained in the same software application this is relatively easy to effect.

Some risks may be transferred to other risks, either existing or new. This happens if a risk changes in nature and becomes bound up with a similar risk, or it is thought better to open a new risk to reflect the new circumstances. The original risk is consequently closed.

Regular review of actions progress will decide whether additional actions are needed for a particular risk. Actions have a tendency to breed further actions, so it is important to ensure that the original actions are effective.

Contingency actions need particular review. They are in place in case a risk impacts, but there is no point in having a disaster recovery plan if it has not been prepared for or tested. 'Will the contingency plan actually work?' is a key question to ask.

Consider the following risk:

Because of the proposed change to employees' working conditions there is a risk that there will be widespread rejection of the proposals, resulting in several legal claims against the company.

Any attempt to change working conditions has to be high risk, so some form of contingency plan would be appropriate. However, until the change is announced the reactions from employees will not be fully known. How do you, therefore, mitigate such a risk?

Firstly, more information needs to be gathered. So, initial actions would need to concentrate on this. The possible areas of objection need to be estimated. There may be previous data for this from other areas of the company or externally – other companies have certainly gone through this activity. Also, the potential damage needs to be estimated – best case, worst case, most likely case. Then, depending on the answer, the risk may be covered by a contingency plan or may be contained through other courses of action, such as the preparation of sample responses to possible objections, bound up in a communications plan, perhaps. Further data is likely to be required, legal counsel may need to be sought, and it may be necessary to test reactions through a confidential sample of employees affected.

Of course, many of these actions should already be tasks on a project plan. The risk mitigation aspect ensures that those actions effectively cover the risk.

This example shows, firstly, how important it is to devise a plan for actions, rather than just assigning actions in a piecemeal fashion, and secondly, how important is the link between mitigation actions and tasks on the project plan.

Effect on the project plan

Each risk action carries a trade-off. No action is for free and the project plan will be impacted in some way. There is only so much time and money available for performing actions and undertaking project tasks. A balance has to be made.

Things to consider are:
- the effort required to undertake the risk action
- the cost required to undertake the risk action
- the cost of not undertaking the risk action (opportunity to avoid future issues may be lost)
- the effect on other work for the person undertaking the risk action
- the importance of the risk action
- how effective the risk action will be (success rate in reducing the risk)
- any saving to be made in the project budget or schedule through undertaking the risk action.

In some cases a change request may be required in order to effect the risk action. In other cases negotiation will be required with other project stakeholders, organisations, mandatory authorities, or departments beyond the organisation's project team.

I prefer to mark tasks on the project plan that specifically relate to risk actions. This ties them back to the risk register, so that if any changes are made on the risk register they can be easily identified and changed on the plan. I know of no software currently that provides an automatic link between the register and the plan.

Chapter 5

Recording risk

Once risks have been identified it is important to be able to refer to them again, so some sort of recording mechanism needs to be established. The risk register is the generally accepted term for the place where risks are recorded, and the risk log is usually the one-line summary of each risk. You will occasionally find the two terms interchangeable, but it is good practice to refer to the detailed record as the register and the summary record as the log.

THE RISK REGISTER

What should a project or programme risk register look like? Well, there are many opinions, and these will often relate to particular company practice. Good practice dictates a core set of recordable elements, however, and these are covered in this chapter. I also recommend additional elements[1]. These are not in widespread use but have proved highly valuable for me during my years as a risk practitioner. I suggest that you do not record more than you need to, however, since this will just create extra work. Think about whether particular elements will ever be needed after you have recorded them: for analysis purposes, by a programme or project office, for example.

Table 7 shows a risk register that I recommend. You will see that

---

[1] Detailed explanations of each risk element are given in the chapters to which they refer.

it is divided into three layers, each separated by a horizontal double line. The top layer deals with the initial identification of a risk. The middle layer is for evaluation of the risk and the bottom layer is for mitigation of the risk.

Dividing the register in this way allows you to record only the necessary information for a risk at its relevant stage in the risk management process. Thus, on identifying a risk, only the top layer needs to be completed. There will be occasions, of course, when all three layers will be completed at once. To derive the most benefit from this register it is important to utilise all the fields over the appropriate stages of risk management.

The risk register is basically the same structure whether it be for use at the project or the programme level. At the programme level, it would be useful to include an additional field to indicate the projects affected.

The risk identification layer

Taking one of the two risks identified in the chapter, 'Identifying risk', we could record it in simple terms as follows:

Risk number	Risk		
R1	Because of a need to add an extra module to the design	there is a risk that systems testing may be late	resulting in a delay to the project schedule

It is helpful to maintain the three separate parts of the risk in individual compartments. This ensures that the cause, risk and effect are brought out in the overall risk statement, and is particularly useful as a guide for team members not used to expressing risk in this way.

Numbering risks enables them to be quickly identified, and is

Total cost of project: _____

Total risk exposure: _____

Risk no.	Sub-project	Area affected	Raised by	Date raised	Risk status

Cause	Risk	Impact
Because of	there is a risk that	resulting in

Prob. %	Impact %	Risk owner	Priority	Risk exposure £K	Impact cost £K	Evaluation comments

Action no.	Mitigation action	Action owner	Priority	Due date	Reduction in prob. %	Reduction in impact %	Cost £K	Action status

Table 7: Sample risk register, incorporating identification, evaluation and mitigation for each risk

an essential component of the risk log, where brevity is all important. The risk log entry for the above might look like this:

Risk number	Risk
R1	Risk that systems testing may be late

There are no rules for risk numbering, but I have seen many elegant interpretations of this requirement. Codes may be used for identifying the sub-project to which the risk refers or for identifying the date it was raised, for example. I quite like an arrangement for the latter, where a date is appended to a unique number. So, R0203001 is the first risk raised in March, 2002. When scanning a log this clearly shows how old the risk is, reminding people of its overdue status, perhaps.

If simplicity is your requirement, 'R1' is perfectly acceptable. (I recommend using the letter R in order to differentiate between a risk and any other project exceptions capable of being numbered, such as an issue (I) or a change (C)).

It is useful to be able to specify the area of the project affected by the risk and, if applicable, the sub-project name. This grouping is helpful when performing risk analysis. Risks can be charted by sub-project and/or focus area. The name of the person who identified the risk is also useful, plus the date it was raised. When a risk owner is assigned later it is helpful for that person to know whom to contact for further information about the risk and the circumstances under which it was raised.

To complete our examination of the top layer (risk identification) you will find it useful to assign a status to the risk. The *Risk Status* field appears in the top layer but, in practice, it applies to all three layers, since the status codes you will assign will change according to the risk's position in the risk management process.

You will find it helpful to select some status codes for use with this field. Your company may have preferred codes, but I like to keep them simple and memorable and relate them to the progress of the risk through the risk management process. Table 8 shows my preferences.

Code	Explanation
NEW	New risk awaiting evaluation
EVALUATED	Evaluated risk awaiting mitigation actions. (It is the risk owner's responsibility to ensure that actions and action owners are assigned)
ACTIONED	Mitigation actions have been assigned
CLOSED	No longer a risk, for whatever reason

Table 8: Risk status codes

Using the risk example in this chapter the risk identification layer might look like this:

Risk no.	Sub-project	Area affected	Raised by	Date raised	Risk status
R0203 001	Systems design	A6 application	Peter Simpson	04 Mar 02	NEW

Cause	Risk	Impact
Because of a need to add an extra module to the design	there is a risk that systems testing may be late	resulting in a delay to the project schedule

The risk evaluation layer

This layer is concerned with assessing the risk's likelihood of occurrence, its impact to the project and the cost of its impact. Risk evaluation can be done at the same time as a risk is identified, though, more typically, it is done later, since it can be a more involved process and require expert input. Often, a risk owner would be assigned, usually from within the project team, whose job would be to ensure that the risk is adequately evaluated. (Refer to the chapter, 'Risk evaluation' for details of the process).

The evaluation layer includes the field *Evaluation comments*. This is useful for anyone re-assessing the risk, since the comments in this field indicate why the risk has been assessed as a particular probability and impact. An example of evaluation comments is given below.

Evaluation comments
Situation has occurred before (ref. XYZ project), so likely to occur again. Impact would severely affect the design stage. Impact cost includes cost of re-designing the ABC component.

The evaluation layer includes some fields that may be quantified: Probability %, Impact %, Impact cost and Risk exposure. These fields work together and can be powerful indicators when used in conjunction with the total cost of the project. I recommend using the following order for inputting these fields:

1. Probability %
2. Impact cost
3. Impact %
4. Risk exposure.

Some people prefer to break out the types of impact cost and differentiate between direct costs and indirect costs. In that case it is easy to specify additional fields.

The register dispenses with the highly inaccurate use of the qualitative values 'High', 'Medium' or 'Low' for evaluating *Probability* or *Impact*. Instead, it requires an estimate of the percentage Probability and Impact.

1. Estimate the likelihood of the risk occurring (1–99%) and put the figure in the field *Probability %*. Note that a probability of 100% is invalid, since it effectively makes the risk an issue. *(See section on 'Probability' in the chapter, 'Evaluating risk')*.
2. Calculate the cost of the impact (for example, in terms of days lost and people resources needed to repair the damage) and enter it in the *Impact cost* field. (Use the *Evaluation comments*

field to give a description of the cost breakdown).

3. Convert this figure to a percentage of the cost of the total project and enter this in the *Impact %* field. (Ensure that an estimate of the total cost of the project is entered in the box at the top of the register). *Impact %* can be any figure from 0%, and can be higher than 100%, of course.

4. Calculate the *Risk exposure* for the risk by multiplying the *Impact cost* by its respective *Probability %* . A Risk exposure for the total project may be calculated by totalling the risk exposures for each risk and placing the total in the box at the top of the risk register. Note that mitigating actions may reduce the figure considerably, after allowing for their cost. *(See the section, 'Calculating the risk exposure' in the chapter, 'Evaluating risk'.)*

You may feel that calculating the *Impact %* is superfluous. However, it is both a useful quick indicator of impact when comparing risks in the register and a useful figure for reporting purposes.

The *Priority* field is available for indicating the importance of the risk. A numerical indication may be used (say, 1, 2 or 3) or qualitative statement, such as high, medium or low. Clearly, the priority would reflect both the probability of the risk occurring and its severity of impact.

Our evaluation layer might now look like this:

Prob. %	Impact %	Risk owner	Priority	Risk exposure £K	Impact cost £K	Evaluation comments
60	5*	Simon Edwards	1	1.8	3.0	2 weeks' delay at £1.5K per week

The above fields probably represent the minimum most useful for evaluating project risks. Some projects may require more sophisticated or company specific measures.

* Total project cost is £60k for this example.

The risk mitigation layer

The risk mitigation layer contains the fields necessary to control the assignment of actions to mitigate or contain the risk.

Each action has a separate action number. I recommend using the same format as for the numbering of the risk itself, but using the designation 'A' instead of 'R'. Alternatively, a more simple numbering may used such as A1, A2, etc., or the action may be tied in with the risk, such as R1/A1 (Action 1 of Risk 1). Whatever method chosen it is important to understand how the actions will be monitored and controlled on a regular basis. It is possible, for example, to control the actions from all the project exceptions together (risks, issues and changes), in which case a suitable identification for each would be required.

The risk mitigation layer also includes fields for estimating the reduction in probability and impact, since it is reasonable to assume that the probability and impact might be reduced as a result of performing some actions. If an action does not reduce one or both of these the risk owner must question whether the action is worthwhile, since performing any action costs time as well as money. However, some zero reduction actions are necessary as preparation for a follow-on action.

The *Priority* field is useful for highlighting which actions should be worked on first. Thus, priority 1 actions would take precedence over priority 2 actions. The amount of probability and impact reduced by completion of an action would have an effect on deciding its priority.

The *Cost* field is for capturing the cost of the action. It is particularly necessary for contingency actions, ie, actions that involve putting something in place in case the risk impacts. (Refer to Action A0203003 in the example opposite).

The *Action owner* field is for specifying the person who will take responsibility for ensuring that an action is carried out. Note that this is not necessarily the person who will undertake the action. A group of people may be required to undertake the action, but it is important to have one person accountable for seeing it all through.

Finally, the *Action Status* field is a useful record of progress against an action. The project manager or project office can use this field to record items from say, a weekly status meeting.

Our sample risk might now look like this in the mitigation layer:

Action no.	Mitigation action	Action owner	Priority	Due date	Reduction in prob.%	Reduction in impact%	Cost £K	Action status
A0203 001	Clarify the need to add an extra module. How certain is the requirement?	Mary Brown	1	01/04/02				01/04/02.Closed. Requirement not certain. Suggest specialist view or outsourcing work
A0203 002	Perform a detailed assessment of the system test plan and identify slack in the schedule	Mary Brown	1	01/04/02		-2%		01/04/02.Closed. Schedule could be reduced by 3-4 days
A0203 003	Devise contingency plan for outsourcing the ABC design work	Karen Johnson	2	29/04/02	-40%		1	

The full register entry for this risk now looks like this:

Risk no.	Sub-project	Area affected	Raised by	Date raised	Risk status
R0203001	Systems design	A6 application	Peter Simpson	04/03/02	ACTIONED

Cause	Risk	Impact
Because of a need to add an extra module to the design	there is a risk that systems testing may be late	resulting in a delay to the project schedule

Prob. %	Impact %	Risk owner	Priority	Risk exposure £K	Impact cost £K	Evaluation comments
60	5*	Simon Edwards	1	1.8	3.0	Two weeks' delay at £1.5K per week

Action no.	Mitigation action	Action owner	Priority	Due date	Reduction in prob.%	Reduction in impact%	Cost £K	Action status
A0203 001	Clarify the need to add an extra module. How certain is the requirement?	Mary Brown	1	01/04/02				01/04/02. Closed. Requirement not certain. Suggest specialist view or outsourcing work
A0203 002	Perform a detailed assessment of the system test plan and identify slack in the schedule	Mary Brown	1	01/04/02		-2%		01/04/02. Closed. Schedule could be reduced by 3-4 days
A0203 003	Devise contingency plan for outsourcing the ABC design work	Karen Johnson	2	29/04/02	-40%		1	

* Total project cost is £60k for this example.

The risk log

The risk log is essentially a one-line summary of each risk in the risk register. As such, it is a very useful aid, for example, at weekly status meetings. Only essential detail is captured, and the choice of what is essential is down to the individual project. If the risk register is automated, then the risk log can be generated automatically. (Table 9 gives an example.) If the risk log is to be of value it needs to be unambiguous. Logs containing a risk number but no description of the risks will be difficult to use, unless everyone has a very good memory!

Automating the register

It is perfectly possible to use a paper-based risk register and log for a small, contained project, but for a larger project it is better to use a computer application. This could be something constructed specially for use as a company standard or it could be an application purchased 'off the shelf'.

Before deciding how to do this, it is worth considering its use and purpose. The register is primarily a vehicle for control. The ability to undertake analysis and produce reports is more important than purely recording the data. I have seen many home-grown registers that have been excellent recording vehicles but have fallen remarkably short on analysis and reporting. In programming terms, these latter tend to be more problematic and time-consuming to construct, so are often poorly contrived.

In a large project it is likely that a project office will maintain the risk register, inputting data and producing regular reports. Access might be granted to individuals, such as risk owners, so that progress on their risks can be updated directly. In this case, it might be beneficial to have a web-based application, which would facilitate easy access from almost anywhere in the world. An interactive application would enable information to be sent to

Risk no	Sub-project	Risk summary	Date raised	Risk status	Risk owner	Prob. %	Impact %	RE $K	Comments
R0201001	Bus. analysis	risk that the business owners will not have time for actions	1-Jan-02	ACTIONED	ASD	60%	8%	8.40	
R0201002	Bus. analysis	risk that data will not be available when needed	1-Jan-02	ACTIONED	ASD	30%	1%	0.60	
R0201003	Communi-cation	risk that roadshows will be delayed	3-Jan-02	ACTIONED	TP	40%	1%	1.20	
R0201004	Communi-cation	risk that field announcement will not be ready before the holiday period	3-Jan-02	CLOSED	TP	30%	6%	6.00	Risk avoided 24.01
R0202001	Test 1	risk that test site will not be ready	3-Feb-02	ACTIONED	LM	60%	6%	6.00	
R0202002	Production	risk of poor quality of components from XYZ	12-Feb-02	EVALUATED	BN	25%	2%	2.00	
R0202003	Production	risk of build failure in module GP376	23-Feb-02	NEW	JJB				

Table 9: Example of entries in a risk log

action owners and risk owners, such as reminders of overdue actions or completion of actions.

For me, an ideal application is one that incorporates risks, issues and changes all in one database. Unfortunately, I know of none that exists off the shelf, though I have constructed them for particular projects. However, such an application would cater for the common element of all these project exceptions – actions. It would also enable a risk to be viewed in context and not as a stand-alone element. The pathway of risks to issues and changes has already been described in the Introduction of this book.

Figures 4,5 and 6 show sample pages from a purpose-built risk register, coded using SQL. The screens are fairly simple in design. As already stated, the complexity is not in the data input, but rather in the analysis and reporting.

Figure 4: Identification page from a purpose-built risk register

Figure 5: Evaluation page from a purpose-built risk register

Figure 6: Actions page from a purpose-built risk register

Chapter 6

Analysing and reporting risk

Risk analysis is the use of risk data to create information that will help make decisions about the project. The information may be in the form of charts, models, lists or reports. A significant amount of data may be accumulated in a project – even more in a programme. There are many ways that this data can be used to provide information. This chapter shows a few that I have found useful for particular purposes.

RISK MODELLING

One of the best ways of analysing risk is to construct a model of risk for your programme or project. There are various methods of modelling risk, but I prefer to use a technique which I call 'risk concept mapping'.

Risk concept mapping

The benefit of this technique is that, for only a few hours' work, a team can have a picture of the worst-case risk that may be encountered during the life of a project or programme, and the events that may lead to it. The resultant map shows pathways from risk drivers to risk events and risk outcomes. It also shows risk increasing in impact towards a final outcome. Because the input to the map is derived from teamwork, its ownership is quickly assured, thus making easier the planning of risk mitigation strategies.

The technique is useful at any stage of a project, but can be commenced well before project start-up. It is particularly powerful at any pre-project bidding stage when a company needs to know the full picture of risk before making a proposal.

Figure 7 shows a risk concept map of possible risk drivers leading to increasing degrees of risk situations and impacts. The risk drivers (squares) are not risks themselves but are possible environments or trigger points for risk. They trigger risk situations (circles, light shade) that give rise to either further risk situations or to risk impacts (circles, dark shade). The risk situations are similar to risk drivers in that they are not themselves risks, except that they describe events or situations that could be triggered by the risk drivers. The impacts tend to increase in severity towards a final, worst-case impact.

The map reads from left to right and is best constructed in a group session. Although it is best to start with the risk drivers, the symbols do not have to be rigidly built-up in order. It is normal, for example, for the team to think of some worst-case impacts before some of the risk situations have been identified. In this case, the impacts can be placed to right of the map, ready for the pathways leading to them to be defined.

The map represents the team's assumptions of the events that could occur in an unconstrained environment. Several iterations may be needed before the map is deemed complete by the project team. The map tends to become stable quite quickly, the risk situations and impacts requiring little alteration over time, thus giving the team confidence in knowing the potential risk they may encounter.

It is possible to relate individual risks to the risk situations. Figure 9 shows how this can be done graphically. This more

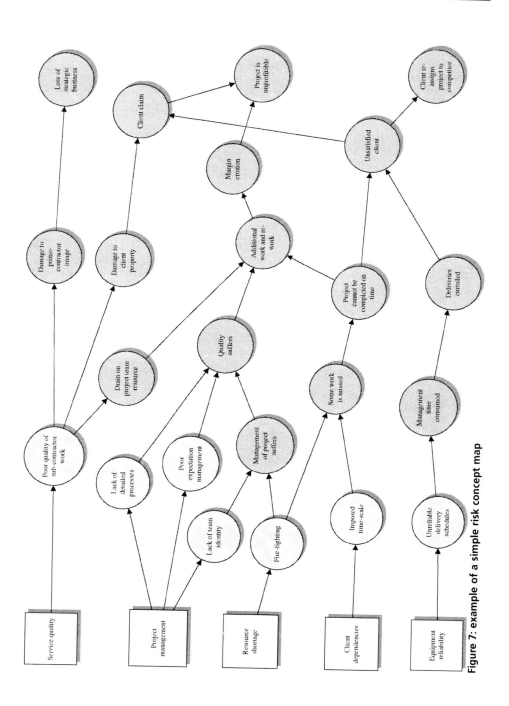

Figure 7: example of a simple risk concept map

detailed map shows risk numbers (small circles) which relate to entries in a risk register. Adding individual risks means that the map will need regular updating. It does, however, show the risks in context. Immediately, it is possible to see which risk situations are associated with several identified risks and which risk situations are associated with very few or none. It is also feasible to add the probabilities to the impacts, and an average could be calculated for all the risks along each pathway.

The risk concept map in Figure 9 also shows hexagons. These represent assumptions about the risk situations and are a useful way of providing supportive information. Assumptions, in this context, are a general use of the word and can be used in several ways. They can aid risk evaluation, since they can state an opinion at the time the map is created that can be validated over time. They can clarify the text in the circles or enhance the argument as in the assumption 'volume testing cannot fully simulate use over time' for the risk situation 'robustness of notes and coins over time has yet to be proven'. They can point to specific instances of a risk situation or impact as in 'local practice' for the risk situation 'different approaches to hardware, software, etc.'. They can suggest a mitigation for a risk situation, as in 'banks need to consider staff incentives' for the situation 'retention of required resources may be difficult and costly'.

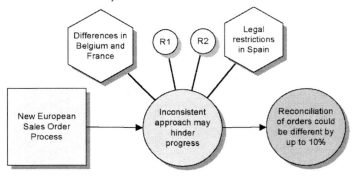

Figure 8: Example of a risk pathway using the full symbol set

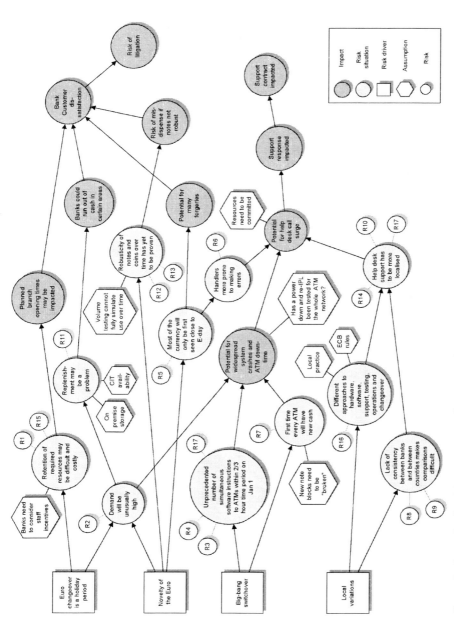

Figure 9: Example of a risk concept map for a Euro changeover project for automated teller machines (courtesy NCR Ltd)

By showing risk in a flow diagram format, some interesting aspects are revealed. Firstly, there is the aspect of clustering. In Figure 9, the impacts 'potential for widespread system crashes', 'potential for help desk call surge' and 'bank customer dissatisfaction' appear as key nodes, since more than one risk situation contributes to each. Many impacts have more than one cause, so clustering helps to identify graphically the causal contributions.

Secondly, risk pathways may be identified. Figure 8 shows a minimal risk pathway using the full symbol set. Where these pathways contribute to other pathways is significant. A stand-alone risk register would not be able to show this easily.

Risk concept maps may be nested. An overall map could represent the risk for an entire programme and lower-level maps could be constructed for individual projects.

Used in conjunction with cause-and-effect diagrams, conceptual risk maps can be a useful means of showing the overall risk picture for a project or programme. Figure 10 shows this combination in use at NCR where I established a 'risk room' for the ATM Euro Conversion Project as part of NCR's preparation for the Euro programme. The 12 participating countries were

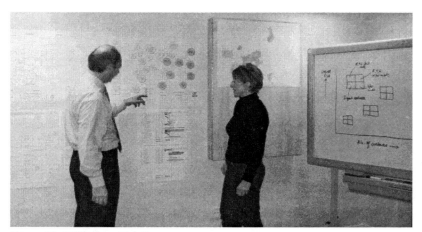

Figure 10: NCR's Euro Risk Room

monitored in terms of conversion readiness and the risk of non-compliance or hardware and software failure was calculated. Four key measures of readiness were tracked (software, support and two types of hardware) and mapped against ATM volumes and the number of customers in each country. The initial risk pathway created gave an early confidence among all parties of the scale of risk. It remained little changed throughout the project, providing a firm basis for monitoring and control.

Cause-and-effect diagrams

Cause-and-effect diagrams (also known as Ishikawa diagrams) show contributors (causes) to a single outcome (impact), whereas the risk concept map can display multiple outcomes. However, the cause-and-effect diagram is a good vehicle for displaying more detail than a risk concept map. It is useful, for example, for showing additional detail for risk pathways leading to a single impact on a risk concept map. Figure 11 demonstrates this for the risk pathways from Figure 9 that lead to the impact 'bank customer dissatisfaction'.

Cause-and-effect diagrams are also useful for investigating a

Figure 11: A single impact from Figure 9 expressed as a cause-and-effect diagram

problem that has occurred, since they can be constructed retrospectively, extrapolating back to the causes of the problem. This is helpful during project close-out when attempting to learn lessons from the project.

Infinite branches may be constructed for each contributing concept, allowing a very fine level of granularity. It is difficult, however, to show interdependencies across the branches. The risk concept map is able to do this well, subject to having too many lines crossing, and so cluttering the map.

The cause-and-effect diagram displays clusters of contributions well. Figure 11 shows that 'Dispensing accuracy' can be shown as a discrete series of branches. Similarly, 'High demand'. This enables the viewer to focus easily on all the causes relating to a single aspect.

Variants of the cause-and-effect diagram described above exist in some industries. These may show the effect as an impact, centrally focused, with a network of causes leading to it from one side and a network of recovery actions leading to it from the other. Similarly, in safety risk practice, this might be an incident as the central focus, with causes and consequences contributing to it.

Influence diagrams and decision trees

Influence diagrams and decision trees are similar types of diagram that show the effect of decisions in relation to chance events. These decisions may be quantified and may lead to one or more numerical outcomes, such as cost, revenue or profit. Several software applications exist to assist the construction of influence diagrams and decision trees.

The influence diagram may have some similarities to the risk concept map in appearance, but it is more aligned to a decision tree in concept, though the decision tree tends to be more structured than the freer format influence diagram.

Whereas the risk concept map models the extent of risk towards ultimate impacts, the influence diagram is able to model how to deal with a risk situation. A diagrammatical difference between a risk concept map and an influence diagram is that the nodes of the influence diagram represent events and decisions rather than situations and impacts.

The influence diagram is useful for indicating possible scenarios for mitigating one or more risks. There do not seem to be any official rules for constructing it, though some software packages adopt a particular format. I like to use the format shown in Figure 12 (overleaf). This example shows three possible decision pathways from a risk event and the relative cost of the decisions towards an ultimate value (pentagons). Each decision (square) is followed by events (circles) that influence the next decision.

Figure 13 shows the symbol set I like to use, though there is no standard. Figure 12 ably depicts the various options for dealing with a particular risk event. A decision tree could show the same options and has the ability to show more detail. So, which is the best diagram to use? Often both are used, but for different purposes. The influence diagram can be a better visual representation of the high-level data, whereas the decision tree can be the supporting statistical evidence. A decision tree also follows a strict chronological order.

Figure 14 shows the same data as Figure 12, but in the decision tree structure. Figure 15 shows a more complex decision tree. Though this example is not quantified, it demonstrates the use of a decision tree for making and testing assumptions. The results of decisions are often two-fold: negative or positive (yes or no).

Decision tree data can be presented in different formats. It can be summarised to good effect, as in Figure 16, where the detailed tree structure might detract from the key points being made. It shows the risk exposures calculated for a new mobile phone product, and the choice between launching the product early to

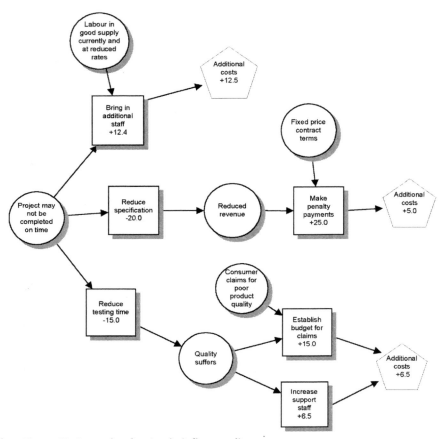

Figure 12: Example of a simple influence diagram

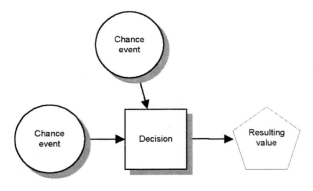

Figure 13: Symbol set for an influence diagram

Figure 14: Decision tree version of Figure 12

achieve competitive edge or delaying launch until further testing had been carried out. The pressures by the business on the project team for the early launch option were considerable, but the result shows the latter option carried the least risk, even though the margin of error in calculating the risk exposures was great. Only the summary risk factors are shown for each option.

Monte Carlo simulation

Monte Carlo simulation is a form of risk modelling that focuses on the likelihood of scheduled dates or budget being met. It may be constructed manually, but this can be quite time consuming, and, today, most charts are constructed using specialist software, either embedded in a planning tool or as a stand-alone application.

A range of possibilities is examined by running several hundred samplings (often known as iterations) of every possible value or outcome to produce a graph showing either the most likely range of costs and the likelihood of completing the project within budget or the most likely duration for the project or projects within a programme.

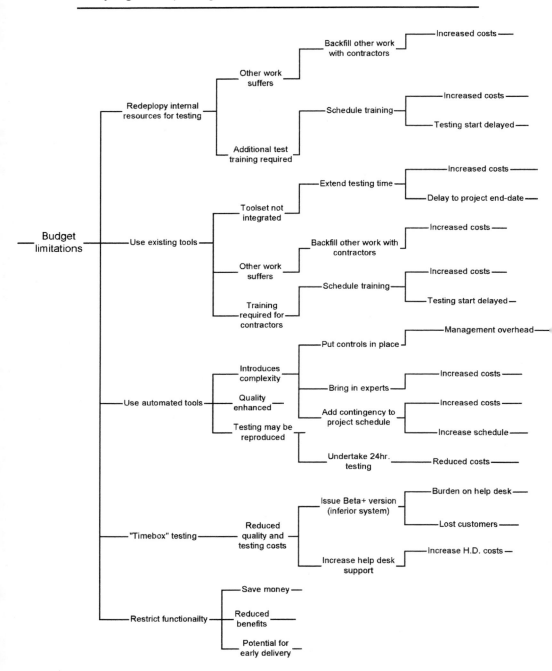

Figure 15: Decision tree with multiple options

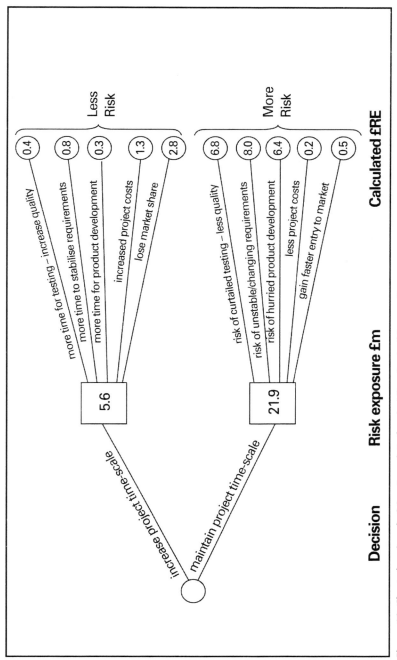

Figure 16: Chart showing decision tree data for deciding best of two options

Probability distributions are used in the calculation, together with any weighted values that a user inputs. The sampling performed relates to the shape of the probability distribution. The distributions have predefined shapes, such as 'triangular', 'normal', 'skewed'. A different result is obtained through both running a different number of iterations and the action of the software's random number generator. The larger the sample the longer the processing and the finer the result. Thus, several thousand iterations should yield a finer result than several hundred. A typical outcome of a simulation is shown in Figure 17. Note the skewed distribution.

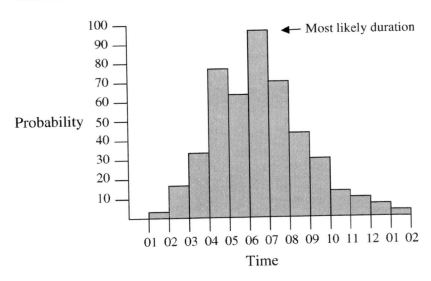

Figure 17: Example of output of a Monte Carlo schedule simulation (triangular distribution)

The Monte Carlo technique simulates a project many times over. This would be extremely difficult for anyone to do manually, so the reliance on software is essential. Using Monte Carlo software it is possible to perform 'what if?' scenarios, altering the input data to cater for different situations.

REPORTING RISK
Reporting considerations

Many project managers forget that the real reason for identifying and dealing with risk is to enable decision-making. Most project decisions should be made on a basis of risk. Therefore, the way in which risk is reported becomes particularly important. Strange then, that risk reporting is not always given the attention it deserves.

In my career I have seen, on the one hand, project reports crammed with pretty risk charts and diagrams, and, on the other hand, reports showing merely a list of risks, none of which enable constructive decision-making. I am not against pretty diagrams, as you can see from the charts in this book, but they do need to be able to convey information upon which decisions can be easily made.

As with all project reporting, it is important to know who is going to use it and what the recipient of the report is expected to do with it. It might be a project sponsor requiring monthly information in order to have advanced warning of potential problems for the business. It might be a project manager requiring weekly information on the likelihood of milestones being met. Whatever the purpose, it is important to produce reports that will be effective. In this section I show some reporting formats that can be useful for particular recipients.

Reporting should be decided prior to project start-up when the project management process is established. The opportunity to include risk reporting within the standard project reporting structure should be taken. I find it beneficial to include risk as part of the general reporting process, rather than as something special and stand-alone. Deciding what to report is an important part of the risk management process. A wealth of data will be collected and recorded in the risk register, and it is wise to make use of that data through analysis and reporting. The risk log, described in the chapter 'Recording risk', makes a good basis for reporting data. It can be used either in its own right as a good summary of individual risks or as selected fields to accompany risk charts. Table 10 gives some indication of the aspects to consider and some possible means of reporting them.

Requirement	Possible reporting vehicles
Establish confidence	Chart of the number of risks by project stage, month on month
	Success rate in number of risks not converted to issues
Reduce risks	Chart showing decrease in both probabilities and number of risks, month on month
Reduce impact	Chart showing decrease in impact costs, month on month
Reduce risk exposure	Risk radar chart used comparatively
Highlight risk severity	Risk ribbon chart with graduated alert status

Table 10: Risk reporting requirements and possible vehicles

Establishing confidence is an important requirement of risk management. Project sponsors, clients, and, in fact, the whole team want to be assured of the successful outcome of a project. The initial risk exposure calculated at project outset may look daunting, but all parties have a vested interest in ensuring that it does not become a reality. Demonstrating confidence may be done through careful reporting. This means showing how the quantity of risks is being reduced for each project stage, week on week or month on month.

A key target is the prevention of issues. This is another

demonstration of confidence. A way of measuring how effectively risk identification is being practised is to track the number of issues being raised that could have been foreseen as risks. Other metrics relating to the practice of the risk management process may be tracked, such as the time taken for risks to be evaluated or actioned. Speed of process is particularly relevant for risk management.

As important as the reduction in the number of risks is a decrease in probability and impact. Some risks may never be eliminated, but a decrease in either probability or impact is just as desirable. This affects the overall risk exposure and, of course, the total cost of the project.

Overall severity (the combination of probability and impact) is a measure that many teams like to report. I find it useful to combine it with an alert status, the categories of which need to be agreed beforehand. It can be helpful in prioritising, especially for projects or programmes where the quantity of risks is great. Here, risks with a project- or business-critical severity are tackled first.

Examples of risk charts

The following are charts I prefer to use at various stages in the risk management process.

Risk radar charts

The risk radar chart is a format I like to use in order to give a steering committee a quick feel for the amount of risk exposure in particular areas. The number of areas on which to focus depends on the nature of the project, but it can be useful to start with those described in the section 'Identifying risk' in the chapter 'Identifying and expressing risk'. Tables 1 and 2 give an example. Figure 18 (overleaf) shows a simple risk radar chart. The chart can be compiled using good charting or spreadsheet software.

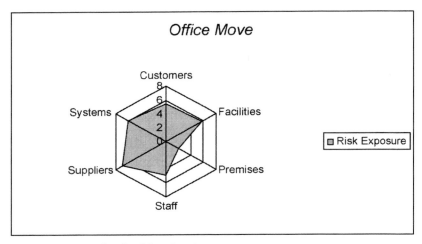

Figure 18: Example of a risk radar chart

This type of chart is highly useful for busy executives with a ten second attention span. It is particularly effective when used in comparison, month on month. I use it mainly for charting risk exposure data, but other parameters may also be used.

Figure 18 is a risk radar chart with the focus areas aligned to the spokes. A more colourful variant is that shown in Figure 19, where the focus areas are aligned to the spaces in between the spokes. In this respect, it is actually a spider chart, and, because it produces a more dramatic effect, it is useful where a particular point needs to be made.

Risk ribbon charts

The risk ribbon chart is a novel way of representing more data and showing its comparison more visually than a standard bar chart. Figure 20 gives an example.

Like the risk radar chart, the ribbon chart may be constructed using good charting and spreadsheet software. In the example in Figure 20, I show the effect of adding a graduated warning key, so

Figure 19: Variation on the risk radar chart

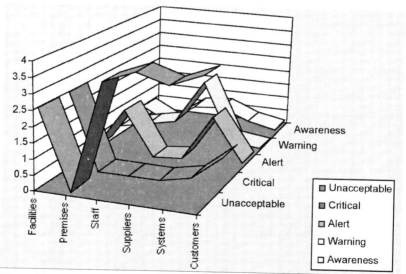

Figure 20: Example of a risk ribbon chart

that an audience may see instantly which areas are giving cause
for concern. It is a nice chart to include in a reporting package

for a project manager. The example shows the number of risks in each area, but other measures such as risk exposure may be shown, of course.

Also, like the risk radar chart, it is beneficial when used in comparison on a regular basis.

Bar charts

Bar charts are useful for showing data quickly and easily. Figures 21 and 22 show their use in depicting the quantity of risks at key project stages.

As you might expect, at contract award, the number of risks identified is high in the early stages (Figure 21). As work progresses to the build stage, the emphasis shifts (Figure 22). Different patterns emerge from different types of project, of course.

The relative height of the bars is a good visual indicator of current status and the simplicity of this type of chart makes it useful for a variety of purposes.

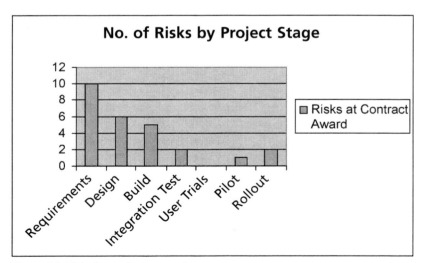

Figure 21: Risks by project stage–1

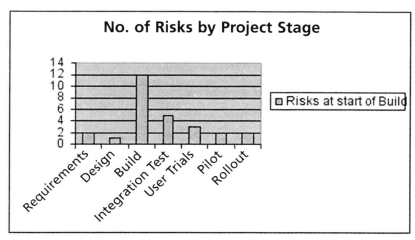

Figure 22: Risks by project stage –2

Probability/impact matrix

This type of chart is a matrix of probability against impact cost and has some use in establishing the priority of risks during risk evaluation, in order to assign actions. The matrix is best constructed using a measure of qualification, such as 'Very High, High, Medium, Low, Very Low'. You will need to convert your percentages of probability to the relevant categories. This can either be a straight apportionment or skewed for those, for example, who rate any probability above 40% as high. *(See the section, 'Probability', in the chapter, 'Evaluating risk'.)*

There are various permutations possible using this matrix, depending on what you want to emphasise. Some people use additional input, which, combined with the probability and impact data, emphasises things such as severity, urgency or cost. Weightings and rankings can also be applied. I prefer to show just the risk exposure. Choose the method that best helps you prioritise the risks. Figure 23 shows an example of the matrix that displays risk exposures in the grid squares.

Health warning: A danger with this type of chart is that it

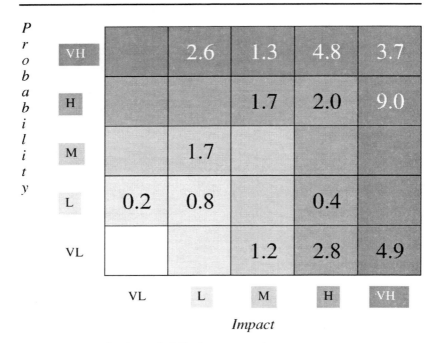

Figure 23: Example of a probability/impact matrix

prompts you to concentrate on the higher quadrants, and there could be a tendency to ignore those risks in the lower quadrants. Sometimes it is the low probability risks that can cause the most disruption; so be careful with the interpretation.

Chapter 7

Managing risk

THE RISK MANAGEMENT PROCESS

The ongoing management of risk should be based around a documented process. This is so that everyone in the team knows what is expected of him or her in terms of risk identification, evaluation, mitigation, reporting and analysis. Most project management methodologies incorporate some form of risk management process and some specify tools and techniques to be used. The exact process to follow, therefore, may be dictated either by a preferred project or programme management methodology or by company standards.

The process of risk management may be divided into discrete cycles, as shown in Figure 24. There are differing views regarding the terminology. For example, some people prefer to call the evaluation of risks 'analysis' or 'quantification' and the mitigation of risks 'planning' or 'risk responses'. Either way, there is no disagreement regarding the cyclical nature of risk management.

Each of the stages is dealt with by a separate chapter in this book. However, some general comments are needed regarding the overall management of risk.

Too often, I have seen risks identified at project outset, but no new risks identified. This practice suggests that both the project

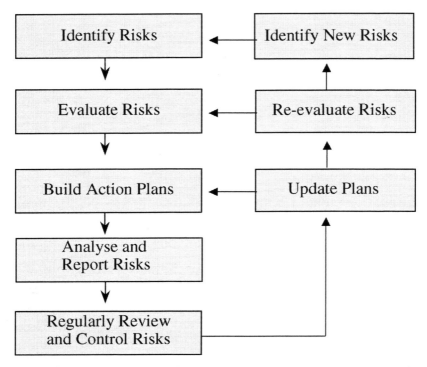

Figure 24: Risk management cycle

and the business environments remain static during the life of the project, which is, of course, just not true. When I audit projects I expect to see a risk register larger than the project issues log. This tells me that new risks are being regularly identified and being prevented from becoming issues by the ongoing practice of good risk management.

In the same way that new risks ought to be regularly identified, so existing risks should be regularly re-evaluated. As work progresses and becomes familiar, the existing estimates of probability and impact are bound to change. A good opportunity to re-evaluate risks, of course, comes when mitigating actions are completed. Their completion should reduce either or both the probability and impact of the risks to which they relate.

Communication is vital for successful risk management, so the risk management process needs to specify who communicates what to whom, how, why and when. Risks need to be visible to the whole project team. The use of a web-enabled tool is ideal for displaying the up-to-the-minute status of risks or for capturing information from members of the team. Too many projects allow no involvement from the team in updating risks, leaving it to a single member of the project office to be in control of the data. Certainly, the risk register needs to be owned by a single person, but inviting input from the team is an important aid to them buying into the process.

The regular involvement of the team can also be brought about through progress reporting. Having risks on the agenda of weekly status meetings, for example, maintains the regular contact between project office, project manager and the team. Weekly status meetings are useful checkpoints for risk, as well as other project exceptions, such as issues and changes.

RISK ROLES

Every team member has a role to play in managing risk, and when I say 'team', I mean the core members plus contributing parties (subcontractors, sponsors, etc.). I have already mentioned the specific roles of risk owner and action owner, which I describe in more detail below.

There is also the more formal role of risk manager. It is a role more commonly found in a programme, but major project undertakings, particularly those that are safety critical, will probably also employ this role. As I stated in the introduction to this book, I feel that project managers do not generally make good risk managers, so the employment of a specialist risk manager is sometimes necessary. The risk management techniques described in this book are appropriate for general project and programme use, but more sophisticated techniques would be required for particular undertakings. It is appropriate to consider the techniques in this book as a good basis for building any additional requirements needed. A good risk manager would be able to build these requirements.

Risk owners

Some aspects of the risk owner role are given in 'Assigning risk owners' in the chapters, 'Evaluating risk' and 'Mitigating risk'. Further details are given here.

The role of the risk owner is to ensure that a risk is properly evaluated and that mitigation and, where necessary, contingency actions are recommended. It is a transient role and can be undertaken by any member of the project team. It is likely in a large project that several members of the project team will act as risk owners during any one period. However, risk owners need to be people with the necessary expertise for owning the risks, since they need to be able to recommend action plans. A risk owner's expertise should be able to identify what actions might be appropriate and who should carry them out, either from direct knowledge or from seeking out those who have the right knowledge. The project manager would make the decision whether it is feasible for the actions to be carried out.

The role requires diplomacy as well as knowledge. Persuading people to act as action owners will inevitably result in close negotiations, and the project manager will probably need to add weight to the argument.

At project status meetings, the risk owners should give an update on the assignment of actions and recommend any change to the risk evaluation. Monitoring the progress of actions can be delegated to the project office, but the interpretation and evaluation of the actions will most likely be done by the risk owners.

Action owners

The risk owners should have a responsibility to ensure that actions are specified for the risks they own. They should also ensure that each action for their risks has an action owner assigned. This may be themselves, depending on the nature of the action, though frequently it is somebody else.

An action owner does not need to be connected directly to a project, so a risk owner must ensure that any action owners assigned outside of a project agree to perform the actions. Action owners may not necessarily carry out the actions themselves, but they should ensure that the most appropriate person does. A departmental head, for example, might be assigned as an action owner, but the action might be carried out by one or more members of the department.

Action owners are responsible for reporting back progress on each action to the risk owners. This ensures not only that someone is accountable for each action, but also prevents actions from being forgotten. It will be necessary to enter certain actions as tasks in the project plan, as the effort in performing them will affect the schedule, the cost base and, possibly, resource demand and allocation.

As actions are completed, risk owners should be able to recommend the re-evaluation of their risks, suitably changing the probability and impact.

The risk manager

The appointment of an experienced risk manager ensures that risk is taken seriously and that it has a professional focus. Particular projects would benefit from this and could justify the overhead. Also, programmes, with their close alignment to a business strategy and their potential to deliver large-scale change, would benefit from this role.

A risk manager would establish the risk management process

and give guidance to individual projects and sub-projects in their identification, assessment and management of risk, offering to facilitate risk identification and assessment workshops and ensuring consistency in the risk management process.

A risk manager must also be able to engage expertise in the identification and assessment of risk and to take a balanced view of its management. Expertise may be drawn from within a project or programme, the company or externally, and a risk manager would probably be the person who would assign risk owners.

A risk manager would also ensure that risks are analysed to defined levels of quality and would decide whether qualitative or quantitative analysis techniques should be used.

The role can be complex and taxing. In a technical programme, the risk manager may be dealing with life-threatening possibilities. A risk manager is usually able to see the 'big picture' and make an overall judgement of the various interdependencies.

Project office

A project administrator is an ideal person to manage the risk register. Either working individually or as part of a project office team, he or she would administer the data in the register, ensuring that it is up to date. Various reports would need to be prepared using the data in the register as a basis. *(See the section, 'Reporting risk', in the chapter 'Analysing and reporting risk'.)*

Figure 25 shows the risk management cycle (dark shaded boxes) together with the main project office risk inputs (light shaded boxes). Essential activities by the project office during the cycle include the monitoring of progress against actions and the chasing of risk owners and action owners for evaluation and action information.

The provision of trigger information (whether automatic or manual) is particularly important for risk owners, and the project office needs to ensure that the process does not lag. This can easily happen if information is not forthcoming for a while. All team members will have other things to do besides risk management, so need regular reminders. A fully automated system can be of benefit, using due dates and calculating optimal time intervals for each stage of the process, but it is no real substitute for the human touch.

The project manager

If there is no risk manager appointed, the project manager would take on some of the responsibilities of the risk manager role. Many project managers understand risk, but are not usually professionally trained risk managers. However, the project manager needs to own the risk management process and be accountable for identifying and managing the risk for his or her project.

In some ways, there is a conflicting mindset between that of risk manager and that of project manager. The risk manager needs to be a lateral thinker, seeing beyond a particular activity by placing it in its business context. The project manager wants to see the bottom line and be assured that schedule, cost and quality will be met.

The project manager will require regular reporting of risk in order to make controlling decisions. Likewise, the project manager will need to make reports to the project sponsor and board, requesting action on exceptional situations.

The project sponsor and board

The project sponsor and board have a key role to play in the management of risk. They will be interested in the overall risk exposure against the budget apportioned for the project. Similarly, a programme sponsor will need to know this for each project within a programme. They will also need to approve exceptional expenditure for the mitigation of risks or contingency plans. In doing this, they need to weigh up the amount of risk they are

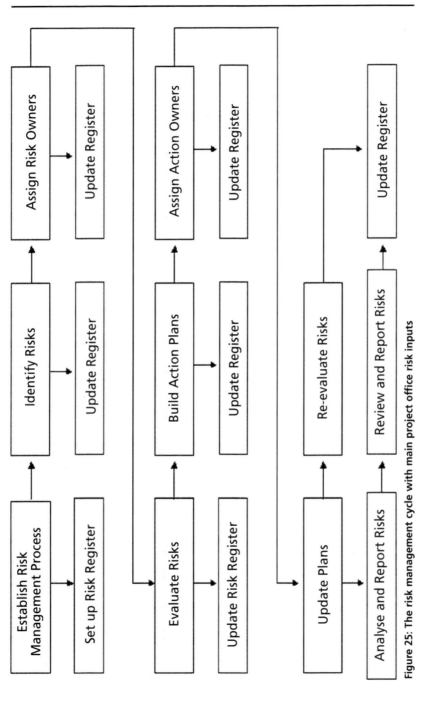

Figure 25: The risk management cycle with main project office risk inputs

prepared to accept and the cost and effect of risk reduction or avoidance against the severity of the impacts. Good data is essential for this type of decision-making, and the project manager needs to ensure that the relevant research and analyses have been made.

The decisions will be more difficult at the programme level. In programmes, the focus on risk in the business environment and marketplace usually has greater significance than at the individual project level. This is partly due to the importance a programme holds within an overall business strategy, but also to the vulnerability of a programme in today's rapidly changing markets and business priorities.

MONITORING AND CONTROLLING RISKS

It is important that the risk management process states the mechanism for identifying and reporting new risks. The whole team should be involved in this activity, and if team members are in a 'risk-thinking' frame of mind then they will take advantage of opportunities to identify risks. These opportunities may occur through progress meetings, site visits, exchanges of email, quality reviews, testing, design and development activities, etc.

The nature of risks will change – some on a daily basis. The risk register needs to be able to reflect these changes. If it becomes a file that is only updated once every few weeks then it will have little value. Changes may result through the performance of actions or the performance of project work. Other changes may arise from the business or marketplace. Monitoring these changes is the responsibility of the risk owners, who need to be able to suggest whether risks should be re-prioritised, split-out, replaced or merged with other risks. Risks are commonly split-out into smaller risks if they become too difficult to manage in their present state.

There is a general view that once a risk becomes identified it stays on the risk register for a considerable time. It is, therefore, easy for risks to become stale. This can be avoided if each risk is regularly reviewed for appropriateness. If it has been too long in a particular status then action may well need to be taken. The pathway from 'identification' to 'actions' should be as short a duration as possible. A full register of actioned risks gives more confidence to the team than one full of risks with a status displaying 'new'.

DEVELOPING 'RISK-THINKING' TEAMS

In the introduction to this book I emphasised the need for team members to be thinking about risk on a daily basis. What does this mean in practice? I believe it means adopting a state of mind that gives overt consideration to risk while undertaking the various project tasks. For example, if designing a piece of user documentation, it means:

- thinking about what is being produced from the reader's point of view. How will it be used? What is the risk of non-acceptance?
- thinking about how the documentation links into other things being developed, such as other user documentation, training and support plans. Who else needs to know about it? What is the risk of being out of alignment with other support objectives?
- thinking about the length of time it will take to develop. What is the risk of not meeting the schedule?
- thinking about the progress to plan and not reporting a risk of non-completion at the last minute. What is the risk of overrun? When should any risk to the completion date be reported?

Risk-thinking is very much about projecting into the minds of others to estimate reactions. Chess players have this ability. It is not just about thinking ahead but thinking about the consequences of future moves.

The more group sessions that can be held to identify, assess or manage risk, the better will be the buy-in to risk-thinking. Regular interaction by the team helps to dispel the view that risk management is a once per quarter exercise.

Creative-thinking techniques have been employed to good effect to encourage a risk-thinking approach. I have used several of these sessions, run by professional trainers, in order to generate ideas in a business process re-engineering programme. The stimulus of right-brained lateral thinking for only a short period was quite remarkable. Ideas flew thick and fast for many days following a session and the vision provided for the identification of risk was noticeably enhanced.

Certainly, I have found that the risk concept mapping technique provides a good stimulus. Not only is it highly interactive but also it is a very creative technique.

Whatever approach is taken to develop risk-thinking it is certainly worthwhile doing so. Risk-thinking does not usually come easily to project teams without a conscious effort to encourage it.

EIGHT THINGS TO GET RIGHT

The best environment for a risk-thinking team practising good risk management is a project or programme where full attention is given to good methodology and leadership. In other words, an environment where plans are produced and maintained, progress meetings are held, changes are managed and all the elements of good project management are practised.

In my book *Managing Programmes of Business Change* I suggested eight things to get right in a programme, all of which are traditional breeding grounds for risk. It is worthwhile repeating these eight things here as they apply equally to all the projects in a programme. There is probably no surprise as to what they are, since they represent good project management practice, so should

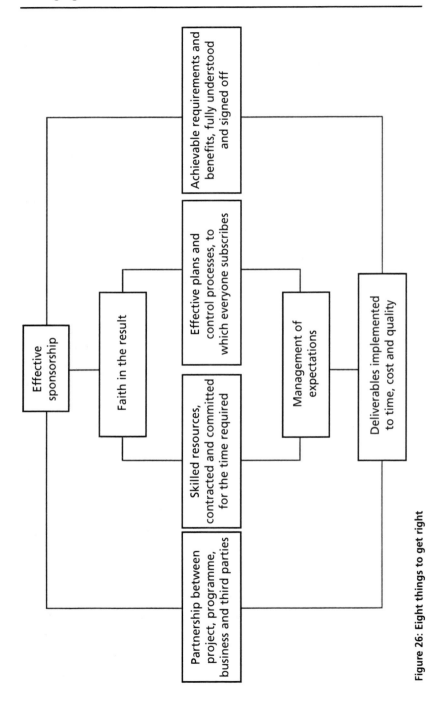

Figure 26: Eight things to get right

really be present in any project methodology. It is by getting these right that risk can be significantly reduced.

Figure 26 shows the eight essentials and presents them as linked requirements. Because they are linked to each other it is necessary to establish all eight, in order to have a chance at achieving project and programme success.

These requirements can be important triggers for risk, some of which can be the causes of spectacular project failings. They are examined in some detail in the next few pages, and can be remembered as the mnemonic PREPARED:

P – Partnership; **R** – Resources; **E** – Expectations; **P** – Plans; **A** – Achievable requirements and benefits; **R** – Result; **E** – Effective Sponsor; **D** – Deliverables.

Lack of partnership

Many projects suffer from protracted conflicts with suppliers and third parties, arising from confusion over scope and deliverables, or misunderstandings concerning resources and timescales, for example. The prime instrument in dealing with third parties is the contract. This is usually the source of any conflict, and is the thing that needs to be right. Legally binding, it is a necessary document, but it can easily sour an otherwise good client/supplier relationship. The enthusiasm of early negotiations between a client and supplier can quickly be dimmed in protracted contractual argument. If suppliers feel the need to refer regularly to their contracts then the contracts have become a barrier to operating as a partnership.

'Risk reward' contracts or joint venture arrangements may be preferable to standard terms for suppliers providing the major part of services to a project. At the very least, documents of understanding should be drawn up which commit suppliers to subscribing to the management processes of the project (ie, the timely submission of progress reports, proper use of and

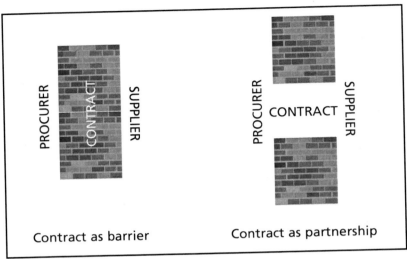

Figure 27: The contractual divide

commitment to the exceptions processes). Figure 27 shows the contractual divide between procurer and supplier, and suggests that a contract need not be a business barrier.

The project cannot afford to carry conflicts of management or politics, yet every large project seems to have its share of these. They are often symptomatic of the business culture and merely transferred to the project environment. The ability to work together for the greater good of the project, without conflict, is a challenging goal, and every project manager's dream, but there are techniques which can help it along. Some of these are:

- Good expectations management, through regular and informed communications
- Documents of understanding between project and business
- 'Road maps' of the project for suppliers and new starters
- Plenary meetings, associated with social events
- Team objectives and rewards
- Proper deployment of resources
- Good working conditions and environment.

Poor commitment of resources

Often cited as the single, largest cause of project failure, the failure to commit resources for the time required is common in large projects, and is usually a sign of inexperienced project organisation and management.

A programme or large project may consume large numbers of resources, some of which will be redirected from existing business operations. This is where the conflicts usually occur, and the risks of resource de-commitments are high. Much is due to poor expectation setting, and line managers can feel a lack of ownership with a project which is currently stealing the limelight.

The project manager or project director needs to establish the right priority of a project within the lines of business, and set expectations of resource requirements. Project managers should be appointed with experience of managing project teams, and 'documents of understanding' need to be drawn up (between line management and project) for all projects in order to commit resources and establish their availability without ambiguity. There must be no doubt between the lines of business and the project as to the importance and priority of committed resources' work.

Increasingly, resources are being utilised externally to projects, with work being contracted out to third parties. Resources are also contracted in, and effective use of this type of resource requires active monitoring. I have witnessed contractors whose contracts have terminated but are still performing key roles. Uncertainties or delays to contract renewal cause loss of productivity. If contractors are spending time looking for their next engagement instead of concentrating on the work in hand then they are not being managed.

The purpose of resources can easily be lost within a large project, and the project office needs to perform capacity planning of resources across all constituent projects to ensure their efficient and cost–effective use.

Poor or unclear expectations

Expectation setting is all about marketing, and is difficult because it is subject to changes in mood and temperament of the targeted audience. For example, in terms of engineering alone the Channel railway tunnel between England and France is a marvellous feat. However, the feat of engineering was overshadowed by the enormous financial difficulties experienced, to the extent that the positive feelings of national pride it sought to exalt were soured by the many negative feelings of a project in deep financial trouble.

There are many examples of elegant technical solutions to business problems that do not gain user acceptance because they do not meet the basic working requirement. Expectation setting is a continual process. It can be accomplished by regular user reviews of work in progress, user councils, prototyping, usability testing, etc. Whatever the method, there has to be no doubt about what is to be delivered and how it is to be used.

Ineffective plans and control processes

The managers of projects and programmes generally understand the need to establish plans and control processes, but the way in which they are utilised makes all the difference. Merely to establish processes and plans and to keep records is inadequate. They have to be effective. That is, the information they contain must be of use to the general operation of the project.

There are many examples of elegant plans being drawn up which fail to alert a project manager to signs of trouble. This is often because the plans are not analysed or planning analysis skills are not present. At the programme level, analysis is fundamental to the tracking operation. The business cannot afford to make decisions slowly, so, accurate, up-to-the-minute management information is vital for steering the programme.

A common problem in projects and programmes is the lack of buy-in to standard processes by suppliers and subcontractors. This results in the failure by third parties to submit regular progress data and to subscribe to the common planning process. Much time is wasted cajoling suppliers for vital information or converting data from inadequate software formats. This is very much a failure by the project manager in persuading suppliers to the importance of the project and their part in its success.

Requirements and benefits not achievable

Important considerations for both project requirements and benefits are:

- that it is possible to achieve them
- that business and user communities comprehend them
- that they are accepted and signed off as viable
- that a rigorous change control process exists.

However, it is often requirements which cause the most friction in projects and programmes. They are more vulnerable to change, and managing requirements change is a particular challenge.

The achievability of requirements and benefits often relates to how realistic they are. 'Blue sky' requirements are a venture into the unknown, often because few but the visionaries understand them. 'Act-of-faith' projects are regularly commissioned, and many have been born out of the '90s vogue for globalisation. These projects stem from an ideal of global trading, cutting across country boundaries and traditions to create the truly global company. Few can say they have been totally successful, and many have cut their losses to embark on more realistic undertakings.

In the information technology sector, many projects and programmes are pioneering in nature, but enlightened organisations have learned to keep such undertakings simple and implement them step by step.

Comprehension of the requirements by all participants in a project is vital, if their translation into completed deliverables is to be effected to the correct design. Sign-offs to design documents and acceptance criteria are also vital, and the principles of change control need to be communicated to everyone involved. I have witnessed ludicrous situations where a project has reached the end of its development phase and requirements have still not been signed off by the business owners.

Lack of faith in the result

The question of faith applies equally to all those who work in a project. A determination to succeed is an important requirement not only for those at the centre of a project but also within its external suppliers. A project whose people have faith in its outcome has a definite buzz. Teams are excited about what they are accomplishing and clearly enjoy being part of it.

When teams lose faith in their ability to deliver the change as planned, morale becomes low and productivity suffers. No amount of incentive can make up for this, and the project manager needs to take regular soundings of morale across the project.

Often, loss of faith emanates from quite mundane things. I once asked a programme team member why he was dissatisfied with working on a particular programme. He replied that the journey to work every day was stressful and fraught with difficulty, and that when he arrived he was accommodated in little more than a shack! This had nothing to do with the nature of the work, which did not get a mention, but the physical environment was rated highly for job satisfaction.

Morale can vary within individual projects, and short-lived projects suffer less from poor morale than longer term projects.

Work in a long-term programme can also be wearing. Some programmes have spanned several years, and ten-year programmes are not unusual, particularly in the public sector. In these situations, there needs to be variety of work and a continual sense of achievement.

Ineffective or unclear sponsorship

The Channel Tunnel, mentioned above, has presented many lessons to be learned from the people, technical and business challenges, owing to the enormous scale of the undertaking. It was not, for example, immune from ineffective or unclear sponsorship. Certainly, the UK Government's insistence on private sponsorship meant that for the crucial early years of the programme there was no single backer or sponsor.

Without a single champion for a project there can be no single vision. Divided visions, from many stakeholders, often mean squabbling, awkward compromises, reduced authority and longer time for decision-making.

The role of sponsor is much misunderstood, and I have witnessed many examples of sponsors appearing in name only. Many projects aim too high in selecting their sponsors. An effective sponsor is not necessarily the chief executive, who may be far too preoccupied to become involved in a project. However, the chief executive may the ideal choice for a company-wide programme, such as preparation for the Euro, since everyone in the company needs to understand that the change is being sanctioned from the very top. However, there is still work to do on the programme's behalf, even for the chief executive, so the role is more than a figurehead.

The sponsor endorses the project and acts as a sort of godfather. The sponsor might appear in publicity material endorsing the project's concepts, or the sponsor might be the first to take delivery of an end-product and demonstrate that if it works for him or her then its good for the business. More importantly, the sponsor champions the cause of the project within the context of the business as a whole. If the sponsor loses faith then the project loses its figurehead, and its direction may be far from secure.

While a programme will benefit from an overall sponsor, each project needs to have its own sponsor. This should ideally be a senior management appointment in the business area concerned, in order to ensure buy-in from that business. Projects which do not have such a sponsor can suffer from a lack of commitment from their business area, which will be tested when, for example, resources are required for user testing tasks.

Deliverables not implemented to planned time, cost and quality

The trio of time, cost and quality are traditional measures of project success, but the question of whether a project is a failure if all three are not met is a question of perception. They are, however, strong contributors, and for many, extremely desirable.

Good planning and estimating will keep a grip on time, and good change control will ensure that 'scope creep' is kept at bay. Scope creep, or the continual widening of a project scope through the piecemeal accommodation of requirements outside change control, is also a contributor to run-away costs. Scope creep is often a contributor to the enormous differences between planned costs and actual costs in several widely reported public projects worldwide. The key question is: Could these costs have been forecast at planning stage, and if so, would any of these projects have ever left the drawing board?

Quality is often a product of both cost and time, and is a particularly elusive goal. Many link the availability of increased time with the opportunity to increase quality, but attach a high cost to achieving quality. The perception of quality as high cost is, of course, false, since quality is merely the meeting of expected standards. The old adage that 'the best things are achieved with time' may have some truth, but there is usually a limit to the amount of testing that any project can undertake, when a decision has to be made that the right quality standard has been reached. The classic project dilemma of 'whether to increase project time to accommodate increased time for testing or to release the deliverables as completed' can only be resolved by analysis of the contributing factors. Figure 16 in the chapter, 'Analysing and reporting risk', shows how a risk analysis approach can provide suitable options for making this type of decision.

DEALING WITH UNCERTAINTY

In business we generally don't like uncertainty. We like to know what we are up against. So, we probe the uncertainties until we reach a point of confidence – but how far do we need to go? 'As far as we need to' is the answer. As a minimum it is necessary to assess the key tasks in the project plan, asking such questions as 'Upon what are they dependent?' and 'What is the likelihood of them being accomplished successfully?' Examining specific areas of the project and searching for risk drivers is another essential activity, not forgetting the environment outside of the project and even outside of the company.

Each company and each project will have its own idea of the importance of risk. Even so, an appreciation of the potential showstoppers is valuable for any project. Achieving the 'eight things to get right' in Figure 26 and understanding the risk influences in Figure 3 are important prerequisites. What you decide to do about them will depend on how seriously you want to manage the risk and how deeply you want to probe.

Take, for example, a task on the plan that requires a third party to develop a vital component, which will be integrated into a product being developed in-house. Various things could go wrong with this task:

- The component could arrive later than scheduled
- The quality of the component could be less than specified
- The wrong specification could be given to the supplier
- The component could fail an integration test into the main product
- The supplier could go into receivership.

Your approach to the validity of these risks and their mitigation would depend on how critical the component was to your project and how likely you believe the risks might occur. Taking the first risk, there are any number of reasons why the component could arrive late. To what extent is it worth checking these reasons?

Let's use the benefit of hindsight and say that the risk of the component arriving late has impacted and that we are now faced with a serious issue. The reason why it was late is because an outbreak of influenza laid low people with all the key skills. Unlucky, you might say. Who could have foreseen that?

Well, the reason for lateness is somewhat irrelevant, since there could have been many factors causing the component to be late – the factory could have flooded, machinery could have failed, to name but two. The point is that if there is a general cause for concern that the component will be late and that each day's delay would cost a significant amount of money, then you would want to mitigate the risk of lateness and probably specify a contingency plan.

You might want to understand the combined effect of all the possible causes in terms of a probability of lateness. Constructing a cause-and-effect diagram might help. Figure 28 shows an example. Probabilities may be added for each branch. Of course, an inspection of the supplier's site could go a long way to assessing the likelihood of many of these risks.

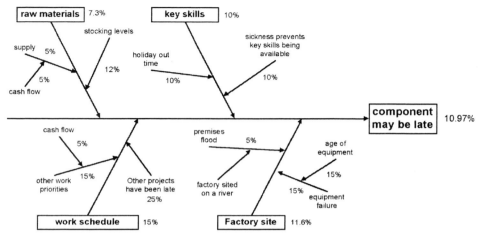

Figure 28: Modelling causes of lateness

The quest for certainty could be taken to extremes. The problem is that we can rarely be certain of probability and impact. Judgements have to be taken and a point of assurance has to be achieved. So, the depth of probing required, the amount of analysis and the time spent on risk management by project resources, all need to be rationalised.

Hopefully, the techniques examined in this book will allow you to select the most appropriate level of granularity for your projects and programmes. I also hope that they will show that risks can be expressed, quantified and managed, and that risk management is not a black art but something that can be practised by all.

Chapter 8

Conclusion

I hope this basic survey of risk management has enabled you to understand how you can confidently employ a good risk management process for your projects and programmes. There is much more that I could have written, but I feel it important not to produce a weighty volume. Rather I have chosen to concentrate on what I consider to be the essential elements of good risk management, providing a few tools for the assessment and reporting of risk, thus enabling its effective management.

The key messages I've tried to convey are that:

1. Risk management is not a mysterious or secretive activity. It can be as practical as project planning once you know how to do it.
2. Risk management is not a negative concept. It can be used positively to improve margins and productivity. Significant opportunities arise through its practice.
3. Everyone in the project team can practise risk management, including customers, suppliers, sponsors and business operations.
4. Risk management is a daily concern, not a once per quarter consideration.
5. Risk management is not a stand-alone activity. It should be part of project reporting, scheduling, issue management,

change management, cost management and quality control, to name but a few.

6. The risk–issue–change pathway is real. Major expense and time can be saved through focusing on risks before they become issues and before they become costly changes.

I wish your projects and programmes success, knowing that from now on risk management will be a major feature in them all.

John Bartlett

Bibliography

Bartlett, John (1998, 2000, 2002), *Managing Programmes of Business Change*. Project Manager Today Publications, 3rd edition, London, 2002. ISBN 1-900391-08-2

Bartlett, John (1992), 'Managing Business Risks in Major IT Projects', APM Journal *Project*

Bartlett, John (1994), *Invest in a Firm Foundation to Manage Risk Throughout a Project*, Proceedings of 12th IPMA World Congress on Project Management, Oslo

CCTA (1995), *Management of Programme Risk,* (John Bartlett for CCTA), HMSO, ISBN:0-11-330672-5

Carter, Bruce, Tony Hancock, Jean-Marc Morin, Ned Robins (1994), *Introducing RISKMAN The European Project Risk Management Methodology,* OPL, ISBN 1-85554-356-7

Checkland, P.B. (1981), *Systems Thinking, Systems Practice*, John Wiley & Sons Ltd, Chichester

Down, Alex, Michael Coleman and Peter Absolon (1994), *Risk Management for Software Projects*, McGraw-Hill, London, ISBN 0-07-707806-0

Hillson, David (2000), 'Project Risks – Identifying Causes, Risks and Effects', *PM Network*, Project Management Institute, Vol. 14, No.9, September 2000, pp. 48-51

Institution of Civil Engineers and the Faculty and Institute of

Actuaries (1998), *RAMP – Risk Analysis and Management for Projects*, Thomas Telford Ltd, ISBN 0-7277-2697-8

Project Management Institute (2000), 'Project Risk Management', Chapter 11 in *A Guide to the Project Management Body of Knowledge 2000 Edition*, Project Management Institute, USA, ISBN 1-880410-23-0

Simon, Peter, David Hillson and Ken Newland (1997), *PRAM – Project Risk Analysis and Management Guide*, APM, ISBN 0-9531590-0-0

Watson, Richard, and Cameron Ramsay: *Focusing Project Risk Management to Enhance Business Performance*, 4th Annual Risk Symposium, London, 11 October 2000 (later re-published in two parts: *Project Manager Today*, April & May 2001)

Wilson, Brian (2000), *Systems: Concepts, Methodologies and Applications*, John Wiley & Sons Ltd, ISBN 0 471 92716 3

Wilson, Brian (2001), *Soft Systems Methodology – Concept Model Building and Its Contribution*, John Wiley & Sons Ltd, Chichester

SUGGESTIONS FOR FURTHER STUDY

In the UK, the Association for Project Management (website: www.apm.org) is a valuable source of information for risk management in a project and programme context. Its Risk Management Specific Interest Group meets to debate current techniques and experiences in the subject, and articles appear regularly in its journal, *Project*. Similarly, the US-based Project Management Institute (PMI) (website: www.pmi.com) also features papers and articles on risk management and has sub-groups (known as chapters) around the world.

The independent magazine, *Project Manager Today*, features

regular risk management articles, and risk management is often a focus for its well-known seminars and conferences (website: pmtoday.co.uk).

The Institute of Risk Management (website: www.theirm.org)is a UK-based professional body dedicated to risk management, providing a forum for the subject, together with certification.

Glossary

Term	Meaning	Chapters
Action owner	Someone who owns an action to address a risk	4
Business	Often used as a generic term for a company's business operation	2
Business case	Business and financial justification for a programme or project	1
Business strategy	A statement of business direction and goals	2
Cause-and-effect diagram	A fish-bone type diagram showing contributing causes to a single outcome	6, 7
Change	An alteration to a project or programme that is exceptional to the current specification, requirements, management, goals or timescale	2
Change control	The logging and control of changes in a project or programme	2
Change management	The high-level management of change in a compan.	1
Change vehicle	A means to accomplish business change. A project is a change vehicle	1
Contingency	An alternative action plan in case a risk impacts, thus avoiding the impact, or an amount of money set aside in case of risk impact	1

Decision tree	A chart of events and decisions designed to aid the choice of suitable options	**6**
Exception	An exceptional event (risk, issue or change) in a project or programme	**1**
Fish-bone diagram	See Cause-and-effect diagram	**6**
Focus area	Sections of a project or business that can be selected for particular attention, to aid risk identification, for example	**2, 6**
Impact	The result of a risk occurring	**3**
Influence diagram	A flow diagram showing decisions in relation to chance events	**6**
Ishikawa diagram	Another name for cause-and-effect diagram	**6**
Issue	An immediate problem requiring resolution	**2**
Mitigation	The lessening of severity of risk through the application of actions	**4**
Monte Carlo simulation	A form of risk modelling to show a range of possible outcomes for dates or costs	**6**
Probability	The likelihood of a risk occurring	**3**
Probability/impact matrix	A chart showing probability against impact	**2, 6**
Programme	A collection of vehicles for change designed to achieve a strategic objective	**1**
Project	A vehicle for change, which is transient and has a defined start and end date	**1**
Radar chart	A type of chart to show the extent of risk in different focus areas	**6**

Ribbon chart	A type of chart to show the extent of risk in 3 dimensions	**6**
Risk	A potential future event that could affect a project or programme	**2**
Risk analysis	The assessment of risk through quantified or qualified means; the modelling of risk data to enable decisions to be made concerning risk in a project	**6**
Risk assessment workshop	A form of workshop designed to enable participants to evaluate risks and plan mitigating actions	**3**
Risk avoidance	Working round a risk so that the risk can no longer impact	**4**
Risk checklist	A list of things to consider when identifying risk, often compiled from previous experience	**1, 2**
Risk concept map	A flow diagram to show situations that could trigger risk, leading to increasing severity of impacts	**6**
Risk evaluation	The qualification and/or quantification of risk, usually in terms of priority, probability and cost of impact	**3**
Risk exposure	A calculation of the cost of risk impacts to a project or programme	**3**
Risk identification workshop	A form of workshop designed to enable participants to identify risks	**2**
Risk management	An umbrella term for the identification, evaluation, mitigation, analysis & control of risk	**7**

Risk modelling	A way of using risk data to predict results	6
Risk log	A one-line summary of each risk from a risk register	5
Risk manager	A member of a project team particularly responsible for the management of risk	7
Risk owner	A person, normally from the project team, who takes ownership for the evaluation and suggestion of mitigating actions for a risk	2, 7
Risk planning	An activity to plan the approach to deal with evaluated risks	1
Risk priority	The importance to the project of a risk in relation to other risks; a signal to tackle the highest priority risks first	3
Risk register	A repository for the recording and control of risk, either paper-based or a software application	5
Risk response	A term used by some to mean the actions planned to deal with identified risks	4
Risk reserves	Money set aside in case risks impact	1
Scope creep	The gradual widening of a project's scope through the addition of changes	7
Severity	In risk terms, a combination of probability and impact	2
Soft systems methodology	A modelling technique for human activity systems developed by Lancaster University in the 1980s	6

Spider chart	A type of chart to show the extent of risk in different focus areas	**6**
Sponsor	A senior manager or executive responsible for acting as business champion for a project or programme	**7**
Steering group	A body responsible for steering the programme	**7**
Tolerance	A range of financial measures by which a project manager has control	**3**

Project Manager Today
P U B L I C A T I O N S

Project Manager Today Publications specialises in books and journals related to project management. Titles include:

- *Managing Smaller Projects*
- *Managing Programmes of Business Change*
- *The Programme & Project Support Office Handbook* vol's 1 & 2
- *Managing Risk for Projects and Programmes*
- *Using PRINCE 2 The Project Manager's Guide*

and the flagship monthly magazine:
Project Manager Today

Publishers of *The Cost Engineer* on behalf of
The Association of Cost Engineers

Full details from:
Project Manager Today Publications
Unit 12, Moor Place Farm, Plough Lane, Bramshill, Hook
Hampshire RG27 0RF
Tel: 0118 932 6665
Fax: 0118 932 6663
www.pmtoday.co.uk

Project Manager Today also organises topical conferences and seminars.